JACOB

Jacob

Unexpected Patriarch

YAIR ZAKOVITCH

Translated from the Hebrew

by Valerie Zakovitch

Yale

UNIVERSITY

PRESS

New Haven and London

Yale University Press books may be purchased in quantity for educational,
business, or promotional use. For information, please e-mail sales.press@yale.edu
(U.S. office) or sales@yaleup.co.uk (U.K. office).

Set in Janson type by Integrated Publishing Solutions.
Printed in the United States of America.

Library of Congress Cataloging-in-Publication Data

Zakovitch, Yair.
[Va-yavo Ya'akov Shalem. English]
Jacob : unexpected patriarch / Yair Zakovitch ; translated from the Hebrew
by Valerie Zakovitch.
p. cm. — (Jewish lives)
Includes bibliographical references and index.
ISBN 978-0-300-14426-0 (cloth : alk. paper)
1. Bible. O.T. Genesis XXXIII, 18–20—Criticism, interpretation, etc.,
Jewish.   2. Jacob (Biblical patriarch)
I. Zakovitch, Valerie.   II. Title.
BS1235.2.Z3713 2012
222'.11092—dc23
2012019478

Catalogue records for this book are available from the Library of Congress
and the British Library.

This paper meets the requirements of ANSI/NISO Z39.48–1992
(Permanence of Paper).

10 9 8 7 6 5 4 3 2 1

For Jeanette and Martin Carr,
with love

CONTENTS

Acknowledgments ix

Introduction 1

1. "The children struggled in her womb":
The Fight for the Birthright 13

2. "He should cheat me twice? He took my
birthright and now he has taken my blessing!":
Jacob the Deceiver 28

3. "And behold, a stairway was set on
the ground and its head reached to the sky":
Jacob's Dream at Bethel 46

4. "It is not the practice in our place":
Wives and Sons, A Mixed Blessing 61

5. "Let me go and I will go to my place and to my land":
Jacob's Odyssey from Slavery to Freedom 76

6. "For you have striven with God
and with men and have prevailed":
Jacob's Homebound Encounters 93

7. "Should our sister be treated like a whore?":
Jacob in Shechem 116

8. "And Isaac breathed his last and died
and was gathered to his kin in ripe old age":
Deaths in the Family 136

9. "And Israel loved Joseph more than all
his sons, for he was the son of his old age":
Priority of the Young 151

10. "Gather together that I may tell you
what is to befall you in the days to come":
An End, A Beginning 169

Conclusion 181

Index 193

ACKNOWLEDGMENTS

I WOULD like to extend my deep appreciation to Professors Anita Shapira and Steven Zipperstein, editors of JEWISH LIVES, for inviting me to contribute to the series and for their helpful guidance along the way. It has been a pleasure working with the superb staff at Yale University Press: Ileene Smith, editor-at-large; her conscientious assistant, John Palmer; the meticulous and ever-encouraging editor, Margaret Otzel; and the extraordinary manuscript editor, Kim Hastings. Finally, I would like to thank my beloved wife, Valerie, for her meticulous reading of my manuscript, for helping me to write for non-Hebrew readers of the Bible, and for her translation, which was done with precision and grace.

Yair Zakovitch
Passover 2012

THE STORY of Israelite history that unfolds in the Pentateuch and Early Prophets stretches from the creation of the
world to the people's exile to Babylon. It describes the relationships between three sides of a (nonequilateral) triangle: the
God of Israel, the people of Israel, and the Land of Israel. The
question emerges: Why would this nation conceive their history as beginning with the creation of the world, the very beginning of time, when only one of the triangle's sides existed?
We could easily imagine beginning the account at another
point, such as the meeting between the people and God in the
wilderness, in the course of which God adopts the wandering
nation as His progeny. This is the version told, for example, in
the Song of Moses in Deuteronomy 32:

> When the Most High gave nations their homes and set the
> divisions of man, He fixed the boundaries of peoples in rela-
> tion to Israel's numbers. For the Lord's portion is His peo-

ple, Jacob His own allotment. He found him in a desert region, in an empty howling waste. He engirded him, watched
over him, guarded him as the pupil of His eye. Like an eagle
who rouses his nestlings, gliding down to his young, so did
He spread His wings and take him, bear him along on His
pinions. (vv 8–11)

A second alternative might have been to open the history with
the commencement of the Israelites' Egyptian sojourn, as do a
number of the historical psalms, for example, Psalm 106: "We
have sinned like our forefathers; we have gone astray, done evil.
Our forefathers in Egypt did not perceive Your wonders; they
did not remember Your abundant love, but rebelled at the sea,
at the Sea of Reeds" (vv 6–7).

The choice of opening with the Creation was also puzzling to a number of rabbinic sages, who are referred to by the
eleventh-century biblical commentator Rabbi Shlomo Itzhaki
(known as Rashi), at the beginning of his Torah commentary:

> Rabbi Isaac said: "The Torah should have begun with 'That
> month is for you the Head of the months' (Exod 12:2),
> which is the first commandment with which Israel was com-
> manded. What was the reason for opening with 'In the be-
> ginning'? Because 'He revealed to His people His powerful
> works, in giving them the heritage of nations' (Ps 111:6),
> that if the nations of the world were to say to Israel, 'You
> are robbers! You conquered the lands of the seven nations
> [of Canaan],' [the Israelites] would say to them, 'The whole
> world belongs to the Holy One, blessed be He. He created
> it and gave it to whomever He saw fit. When it was His will,
> He gave it to them. When it was His will, He took it from
> them and gave it to us.'"

Rashi's explanation seems both incomplete and arbitrary. To
respond, we should probably add, first, another question: Why
do the nation's forefathers take so long to step onto the stage of

history? Were they hibernating while the rest of humanity had already awakened to the dawn of history? Consider that when Abraham, the forefather of the Hebrew nation, and his wife Sarah take their first, hesitant steps onto the proverbial stage, there already existed, according to the Book of Genesis, sizable and developed nations, societies ruled by powerful kings.

The answer, according to the Hebrew Bible, is that a deliberate hand prevented the Israelites from entering the world prematurely, and it did so in order that they might learn from the experiences of others—in order to recognize how the earlier generations paid for their sins against God and to draw the relevant conclusions from these events, from the expulsion from Eden because of Adam and Eve's eating the fruit of the Tree of Knowledge (Gen 3) to the dispersion of the world's population and the confusion of languages following a failed attempt to build a tower with its top reaching to heaven (11:1–9). Indeed, for these actions of the ancients—for these attempts to be like God—the first generations were punished with exile. And truly: had the Israelites learned from the past, they might have avoided the exile that awaits them at the end of the Book of Kings. Instead, they closed their eyes from seeing and sealed their ears from hearing and troubles befell them. Signs that hung in the air from the earliest days of Genesis are then realized in the grim reality of the destruction of the Kingdoms of Israel and Judah, and all who disregarded the warnings implicit from the earliest days will now, perhaps, begin to comprehend that the justice of God's dominion is in both the distant past and the bitter present.

The opening chapters of Genesis also assign Israel's place in the "Book of the line of Adam" (5:1) and, actually, in the "line of the sons of Noah" (10:1), where we learn how Canaan—the eponym of the land in which the nation will later dwell—was a descendant of Noah's son Ham (v 6), while Abraham, the forefather of the Israelites, is a son of Noah's other

3

son, Shem (11:10 ff.). The genealogy teaches how Israel shares nothing with the nation whose land will come to be theirs. All this was designed to dissociate the Israelites from those whom they resembled most, and to argue for the uniqueness of Israelite culture. Indeed, the Bible's historical books are crucial components of the Monotheistic Manifesto, the programmatic statement and argument for the belief in one God that is the Hebrew Bible, which sought to disengage and remove the Israelites from the culture and beliefs of Canaan, a nation still caught in the swampy mires of polytheism.

Understanding this function and purpose of the first stories in Genesis pushes us, next, to inquire why the storytellers bother with the biographies of the nation's patriarchs: Why not proceed directly from the creation of the world to the Exodus from Egypt—the ultimate event that transforms the Israelites into a great and numerous nation ready to take its place in history alongside other nations? The two megaevents in the Bible are the Creation and the Exodus balanced opposite. Suffice it to observe that, while the commandment to keep the Sabbath that appears in the Book of Exodus is justified by the Creation—"For in six days the Lord made heaven and earth and sea, and all that is in them, and He rested on the seventh day; therefore the Lord blessed the Sabbath day and hallowed it" (20:11)—in Deuteronomy the justification is rooted in the Exodus from Egypt: "Remember that you were a slave in the land of Egypt and the Lord your God freed you from there with a mighty hand and an outstretched arm; therefore the Lord your God has commanded you to observe the Sabbath day" (5:15). In another example we notice how a psalm that praises God for His gracious acts skips all events between the Creation (to be more exact, the creation of the heavenly lights) and the plague of the killing of the firstborn, which precipitated the Exodus: " . . . Who made the great lights . . . the sun to dominate the day . . . the moon and the stars to dominate the night . . . who struck

Egypt through their first-born . . . and brought Israel out of their midst . . ." (Ps 136:7–11). If we can jump coherently from the Creation to the Exodus, then what is the purpose of the patriarchal stories? How is the greater historical concept served by these family tales about Abraham and Sarah, their children and their wanderings in and about the Land of Canaan?

The Bible aimed to draw an isolationist picture of "a people that dwells apart, not reckoned among the nations" (Num 23:9). It sought to root out from Israel Canaan and its culture, to claim that the Israelites were not part of the Canaanite nation and that their patriarch Abraham arrived in Canaan from afar, after answering a divine command and passing the first test that God placed before him: "Go forth from your land and from your birthplace and from your father's house to the land that I will show you" (Gen 12:1). Once Abraham arrives in the Land of Canaan, he and his descendants live in almost splendid isolation, having few encounters with the land's inhabitants before leaving for Egypt, where they live apart, in their own territory in the land of Goshen, until they leave for the desert wilderness, for the cultural vacuum in which they will receive their remarkable and unique laws that forbid them from worshiping other gods.

What, therefore, is the significance of the period of the patriarchs' sojourn in Canaan? One answer we may offer is that when the Israelites finally arrive at Canaan's threshold and proceed to conquer it, it is not as invaders, as a nation conquering a foreign land, but as a people who returns to its land, a land that God had repeatedly promised to its ancestors. Through the patriarchal stories, the Israelites' conquest of the land reveals itself not as an aggressive, whimsical fancy of a God wishing to remove the land from its Canaanite residents and reassign it to the Israelites (a view reflected in the midrash and Rashi) but as the result of the law of requital and justice, of divine retribution. The Israelites were promised the land but must wait four hundred years in Egypt before being allowed to enter it, as dictated by God to Abraham in Genesis 15, the Covenant between the Pieces—"for the iniquity of the Amorites is not yet complete" (v 16)—a faint warning to the Israelites (which they fail to heed) that their right to the land is conditional, and that it can be denied them, too, should they sin against God.

The people will return from Egypt not only to the land promised them but to the land in which their forefathers lived, wandered, and left physical traces, where they had been visited by God and His angels, essentially carving a map of its holy places. The forefathers' descendants will therefore return to a land brimming with memories and holy sites, witnesses to ancient encounters between God and their ancestors.

What's more, even a rough sketch of the patriarchs' wanderings coincides with the broad lines traced by later generations. Canaan is located between the two great powers of Mesopotamia and Egypt, and the patriarchs make their way between the three points: Mesopotamia, Canaan, and Egypt. Abraham sets out from Mesopotamia and arrives in Canaan. Before much time passes, he descends to Egypt and then returns to Canaan (Gen 12:20–13:1). His son Isaac never leaves Canaan, but his grandson Jacob, the hero of our book, leaves for Mesopotamia, for Haran, the city from which his grandfather had originally set out (28:10), and returns from there after a twenty-year exile (32:23 ff.); at the end of his life Jacob travels with his entire household to Egypt to unite with his son Joseph (46:7 ff.). These perambulations will subsequently reach their conclusion when the generation that leaves Egypt returns to Canaan led by Joshua ben Nun. In the bitter, final chapters of the Book of Kings, however, the people return once more to Mesopotamia when the inhabitants of the Kingdom of Israel are exiled to Assyria (2 Kings 17:6), and the pattern of wandering is completed later, with the exile of the people of Judah to Babylon (25:21).

What we can—and are expected to—learn from this scheme is that the patriarchs' wanderings were not haphazard; they were not the consequence of some irrepressible urge to travel but manifestations of the trials with which God tested the patriarchs and of the consequences of divine retribution, which will create later waves of exile and wanderings too. God, the dominant side of our triangle, pays close attention to the actions of the patriarchs and their failures and does not hesitate to punish them, clearly demonstrating that divine retribution (plainly apparent in the first chapters of Genesis) is present and functioning in the patriarchal period, too, and will continue to be a force in the generations that follow.

In this book, we recount the life story of the third of Israel's patriarchs, Jacob, from his birth (Gen 25:19–26) to his death and burial (49:33–50:14). Writing a biography in the usual sense is not possible, however, when the subject is a biblical character. The biographer of a contemporary leader will typically have a plethora of diverse and disparate sources available, including those written by the subject: diaries and journals, letters, speeches, or sermons. He or she may have access to news coverage in which the subject's activities are described and perhaps evaluated, letters written to the figure, as well as a bounty of documents and official papers, photographs, and even video footage that may document the subject's involvement in both historic events and the everyday routine of life. In addition, the circumstances surrounding the writing or creation of most of these sources are accessible and readily known, as are, most likely, the dates of the same sources. The proficient biographer sifts through this surplus of sources and chooses from among them, trying to create an objective picture that is complete and as faithful as possible to historical reality.

One who aims to record the life of a biblical figure—namely, one of the earliest of the Bible's characters who is mentioned nowhere outside it—is practically limited to a single source, the story that is recorded within the Bible's pages. Is such a biography even possible? The wise writer is forced to scrutinize the Bible's verses under a microscope, where the unity of the story that begins with Jacob's birth and ends with his death is revealed to be largely an illusion, the product of artistic editing. The Bible's biographies are not magnificent portrayals painted by artists onto canvas but the work of a mosaic-maker who selected, fashioned, and arranged colorful stones until a well-planned and deliberate work emerged. This mosaic merits our acknowledgment and esteem: its creator transformed a collection of stones into a complete work that expresses his ideological world and his estimation of the figure. At the same time, the biographer mustn't ignore the stages that preceded the mosaic-maker's work, the stages in which the individual stones were formed. These small pieces were created and shaped in different locations and historical periods, and they reflect a wide array of ideological movements. The biographer would do well, therefore—and I now exchange one metaphor for another—to listen first to the glorious music produced by the orchestra that plays, for instance, Beethoven's Fifth Symphony, but then that biographer must return to listen to the work harmony by harmony, instrument by instrument, before evaluating each part's contribution to the whole. Moreover, when disassembling the whole, one cannot indulge oneself by listening only to the dominant sounds, such as the violins, but must listen also for the quieter parts, since these faintest voices may give sound to views silenced by the strength of the dominant ideologies. Whoever desires to reconstruct the complete array of voices would do well to listen, too, for these smaller rivulets of tradition.

I've mentioned the term "reconstruct," a notion that warrants consideration. Is it possible to read between the lines of a text and reconstruct a tradition that was rejected, or changed beyond recognition, because it was unwanted? Because it no longer suited the world of beliefs and ideas of the writer or editor? I am convinced that the answer is yes, and I am assisted by the methodology of *literary archaeology*, which can penetrate the recesses of literary history, reaching even the stage of oral transmission that preceded the traditions' being recorded in writing. Reconstructing unknown traditions can be accomplished by a number of means, the most important being the identification of duplicate traditions within the Bible: sometimes more than one version of an event can be found. Examining these duplicate traditions may reveal tensions between older elements and those created to cope with them, to obscure or even replace them. Sometimes the tradition that the Bible wished to reject can be found in the margins, in the textual periphery; sometimes the rejected, twin tradition is even outside the historiographical cluster—in our case, outside the life story of Jacob found in the Book of Genesis—and will be discovered in other biblical genres, such as prophetic literature. Traditions about another figure that parallel what is told about our subject may also aid in reconstructing an older tradition.

Biblical stories' later reincarnations outside the pages of the Bible can also prove instrumental in reconstructing ancient traditions. The vast world of literature that was erected on the Bible's foundation—Jewish Hellenistic literature, the Apocrypha and Pseudepigrapha, the Dead Sea Scrolls, the New Testament, and rabbinic literature in its various manifestations—often preserve ancient, essential elements that were spurned by the Bible. The Bible's writers were powerless to eradicate these elements completely, however. Traditions that the Bible ignored could continue to make their way orally until they no longer presented a danger to a believer's faith or some ideological worldview and then resurfaced in a written text. Here we see the difference between literary archaeology and archaeology involving dirt and rocks: a traditional archaeologist digs deeper and deeper into the earth to reach the earliest layers, while literary archaeologists may uncover ancient elements in later, younger strata of literary tradition.

Biblical literary genres outside Genesis and the Bible's other historiographic writings have, as I've said, preserved elements of earlier traditions. But they are valuable for another reason as well, in that they enable us to look through the ideological lenses of later writers, to understand the way the Jacob stories were read and how the figure of Jacob was perceived by later generations. For example, we will see how Israel's prophets, who saw in the patriarch Jacob-Israel an archetype for the image of the whole nation, kneaded and interpreted Genesis's Jacob stories and adapted them to their needs, to convictions they wished to express. Such free interpretation and adaptation of the ancient texts for contemporary needs is what we call "midrash." Indeed, midrash is not solely the legacy of postbiblical generations: as we will see throughout this book, its earliest expressions can be found in the Bible itself.

Jacob, the hero of this volume, is depicted in the Torah as the son of Isaac and the grandson of Abraham. Is this a convincing image, or will our readings in the Book of Genesis reveal the connection of the three patriarchs to be artificial, the result of efforts to unite various ethnic elements, inhabitants of different geographical areas, into one nation? (A common past, a common denominator, is a condition for the creation of a nation.) Following the footprints of the patriarchs over different geographic areas in the Land of Israel and in different sites may bring us closer to a reliable answer.

I admit that my choice to write a biography of Jacob owes to his being a fascinating figure whose character takes on depth and complexity and whose life is marked by the vagaries of fate. Jacob is no model of virtue, which leads us to ask how a figure with a questionable moral code, a man who does not reject availing himself of deceit and dishonesty, came to occupy a prime position among the nation's patriarchs. The answer is that the Bible—and, principally, those parts of the Bible that were written in the First Temple Period—eschews the depiction of ideal figures for two reasons: first, because saints are liable to invite veneration, personality cults, and thereby cast a shadow onto their Creator; and second, and more importantly, because we, who are not flawless, cannot learn from perfect creatures. The Bible's aim is to educate its readers, and such an education is possible precisely when its figures are not beyond reproach. Thus the Bible's heroes sin and transgress "for there is no man who does not sin" (1 Kings 8:46), and they pay for their mistakes and transgressions like every other. Jacob's life story is one of crime and punishment; of crimes and punishments with compounded interest, in fact, along with lessons drawn and behavior modified. The astute reader learns from the experiences of the biblical characters to avoid repeating their mistakes and thus precludes inviting punishment on him- or herself.

Jacob's enthralling life story, with its many vicissitudes and travels between Canaan, Haran, and Egypt, is but one example, albeit rich and clear, of the Bible's method of depicting the history of Israel by way of a series of biographies, a relay race in which figures receive the baton from their predecessors and pass it on to their successors. The decision to fashion history in this way stems from the interest that personal stories awaken, from the human penchant for identifying with extraordinary figures, and from the hope that this curiosity and identification will cause us to integrate the Bible's messages: that the law of divine retribution is at work, that someone is keeping accounts, rewarding those who do good and penalizing those who transgress. Indeed, Jacob's sins are obvious to all, and he is appropriately punished for them; and yet despite this, we will come to see that in the stories about Jacob another—opposing—force is at work, balancing the first. We will find, both in the stories themselves and in the work of the editors, that efforts were made to show Jacob's merit, to find extenuating circumstances to obscure the darker side of his character and its manifestations. Someone who had difficulty accepting that the nation's patriarch—who was created in the people's image and after their likeness—grievously transgressed sought to improve his image a bit, to make it easier for the people of Israel to accept him as their patriarch. The balance struck between these opposing forces in the biblical account of Jacob's life adds depth to his character.

The last of the nation's patriarchs and the father of twelve sons and one daughter, Jacob stands at the junction at which the life of one family becomes transformed into the history of a nation. The varied traditions that express and serve different motives, and the richly colored mosaic created by their combination, teach us how Jacob's actions, his failures, and God's judgment all served the great, divine plan of transforming Jacob into Israel, the patriarch of the people of Israel.

1

"The children struggled in her womb": The Fight for the Birthright

WHEN THE time arrived for Isaac to wed, Abraham sent a servant to find a bride for his son in Haran, his homeland, since a local, Canaanite woman was unacceptable (Gen 24:3; this derives from the Pentateuch's isolationist ideology). On arriving in Haran the servant, aware of the enormous responsibility entrusted him, wants a sign from God that will signal a woman worthy of his master's son. Standing by a well, he prays:

> Oh Lord, God of my master Abraham, grant me good fortune this day, and deal graciously with my master Abraham. Here I stand by the spring as the daughters of the townsmen come out to draw water; let the maiden to whom I say, "Pray, lower your jar that I may drink," and who replies, "Drink, and I shall also water your camels"—let her be the one whom You have decreed for Your servant Isaac. Thereby shall I know that You have dealt graciously with my master. (vv 12–14)

The sign is granted almost instantaneously: before the prayer's final words have left his mouth, a handsome maiden, Rebekah, daughter of Bethuel, son of Abraham's brother Nahor, arrives at the well and lowers a jar from her shoulder. Her response to the servant's request for water exceeds his hopes when she offers water to his camels "until they finish drinking" (v 18). The servant is received generously by the young woman's father and her brother Laban, who perceive the hand of God moving behind the events (v 50), and Rebekah is willing to accompany the servant back to Canaan, where he brings her to Isaac. At this point, this chapter in the history of the patriarchs comes to the desired conclusion: "Isaac then brought her into the tent of his mother Sarah, and he took Rebekah as his wife. Isaac loved her, and thus found comfort after his mother's death" (v 67).

The story of the birth of Isaac and Rebekah's sons is preceded by a chronological report of the patriarch's age at the time of his marriage: "Isaac was forty years old when he took to wife Rebekah daughter of Bethuel the Aramean of Paddan-Aram, sister of Laban the Aramean" (25:20). (Whoever inserted this verse, whether writer or editor, was not the same person who penned the birth story that follows, but its effect is considerable, as will soon become clear.) The next verse reveals important information about the future matriarch: "Isaac pleaded with the Lord on behalf of his wife, because she was barren . . ." (v 21). Like Abraham's wife Sarah, Isaac's wife is barren—as will be Jacob's beloved wife, Rachel—leading one to suspect that no biblical hero is truly certified unless his mother conceived him following an extended period of infertility. This is because the birth stories of the Bible's heroes require a miracle, and that miracle takes the form of God's intervention in opening the woman's womb. Unlike Sarah, however, who tried to maneuver around her barren fate when she supplied Abraham with her Egyptian maidservant to bear children who would be considered Sarah's own (Gen 16), Isaac knows that the power to open wombs is God's alone, and so he prays. The end of the verse that tells of Isaac's prayer even creates the impression that Isaac had barely finished praying when "the Lord responded to his plea and his wife Rebekah conceived." But verse 26—another chronological verse given us by the same hand that penned verse 20—makes clear that, in fact, twenty years have passed between Isaac and Rebekah's marriage and the birth of their sons, Jacob and Esau: "Isaac was sixty years old when they were born." It is to their credit that, throughout the long wait, the couple placed their full trust in God.

In contrast to other stories about barren women who finally conceive (Sarah, Rachel, Samson's mother, and Hannah, mother of Samuel), our storyteller spares no words for the opening of Rebekah's womb nor does he tell of any announcement to the parents about the impending birth, whether by angels or a vision. Our storyteller doesn't want to distract us with miracles but rather to tell us the more significant news: Rebekah carries in her womb not one child but two.

This news hints at possible fraternal conflict, following a tendency that already runs in the family. Abraham, Jacob's grandfather, parted from his cousin Lot in order to escape the rivalry between them, and suggested dividing the land (13:5–12). Next, Abraham's son Ishmael and Ishmael's mother, Hagar, Abraham's concubine, were expelled because of Sarah's resolve that "the son of that slave shall not share in the inheritance with my son Isaac" (21:10), thereby ensuring the less-than-amicable separation of the two. Overt conflict was thus avoided in both cases. Now, however, with the rivals being twin sons of the same mother, a furious battle between them begins even before birth: "but the children struggled in her womb" (v 22). This is a presage of what is to come. The verse prompts us to think of the friction between the antediluvian brothers Cain and Abel and its terrible outcome, and we begin to fear that the present rivalry, too, will end in tragedy.

Rebekah's response to her sons' scuffle in utero is twofold. She first asks herself, "If so, why am I [alive]?" (v 22; the word in brackets is preserved in the Old Syriac translation of the Bible, the Peshitta)—seemingly prophetic words. (Their fulfillment is discussed in chapter 8.) Next, Rebekah turns "to inquire of the Lord" (v 22). The mother-to-be expects an explanation from God and it arrives, in the form of a poetic oracle:

> Two nations are in your womb
> > Two peoples shall issue from your loins.
> One people shall be mightier than the other,
> > Older younger shall serve. (v 23)

The oracle indicates that the twins' birth will not be of the ordinary sort but will mark the birth of the progenitors of two nations, Israel and Edom. The second stich informs us that the two will fail to live in harmony and will be separate. The second half of the oracle makes clear that their parting will not be amicable and that the brothers will continue to struggle until one prevails over the other. The oracle's final words sound like its Delphic counterpart, and can be understood in contrary ways: the older will be served by the younger (an extraposed sentence) or, alternatively, the older will serve the younger. The medieval commentator Radak (the acronym for Rabbi David Kimḥi) wrote: "the word 'et [the Hebrew object signifier], which shows which is the object, is not mentioned. The matter is dubious. It wasn't made clear who would serve the other, the older the younger, or the younger the older . . ."

Rashi, in contrast, explained the verse's vagueness to mean that sometimes one brother would prevail, sometimes the other—"they will not be equal in power, when one rises the other falls . . ."—that is, the verse's contrary readings reflect the vicissitudes that would characterize future power relations between the nations of Edom and Israel. Another reason for the verse's lack of decisive clarity was so that it would serve as both a prefiguration and an illumination of Jacob's subsequent behavior in the story of the buying of the birthright (told later, in vv 27–34) as well as of Rebekah's actions, which cause Isaac to bless Jacob and not the intended Esau.

The words used in the very next verse convey surprise— "When her time to give birth was at hand, behold! There were twins in her womb" (v 24)—as though nothing had been known previously of the twofold story developing in her swelling middle. This incongruity suggests strongly that, in the original version of our story, verse 24 directly followed verse 21 and read: " . . . and his wife Rebekah conceived. When her time to give birth was at hand, behold! There were twins in her womb." As we will see, the intervening verses, 22 and 23, which relate the brothers' struggle, the mother's complaint, and the divine announcement, were added by a writer whose eye was on the continuation of Jacob's story, on the story of the birthright and blessing.

The existence of twins becomes known, therefore, only at their birth, when "the first one emerged red, like a hairy mantle all over; so they named him Esau" (v 25). Esau is the forefather of the nation that is called both Edom and Seir (Gen 36:8). In order to give expression to all three names, the storyteller explains both that he emerged "red" (*'admoni*), an allusion to the name Edom, and that he was "like a hairy mantle" (*ke'aderet se'ar*), an allusion to the name Seir. The third name given upon his birth, Esau, is not explained.

Immediately afterward the second brother, the patriarch Jacob, is born: "Then his brother emerged, holding on to the heel of Esau; so they named him Jacob" (v 26). At this point Jacob is given only one name, *ya'aqov*, which is explained as relating to his having emerged clinging to the heel (*'aqev*) of his brother. But why, we must ask, did Jacob hold his brother's heel? Might this have been a final, desperate attempt to delay his brother's birth, to pull him back so that Jacob might be born first? This explanation of Jacob's grip on Esau's heel could also explain the nature of the brothers' prebirth struggle: it was a fight for the birthright. And in fact we find this explanation stated explicitly in the midrash: " . . . What is the meaning of 'struggled'? That they would ascend and descend inside her . . . this one saying, 'I will come out first,' and this one saying, 'I will come out first'" (*Midrash HaGadol* on Genesis 25:22).

Biblical name etymologies are not offered naively, however, and were often used to convey significant interpretative information. Some were even fierce—albeit covert—arguments against another interpretation of the name, one that the biblical writer wanted to refute. This seems to have been the case with Jacob and the "heel" explanation. The prophet Hosea blamed the nation, the descendants of Jacob, with deceit, and gave a different explanation of the patriarch's name when he cried, "in the womb he deceived ['*aqav*] his brother" (12:4): for Hosea, Jacob was named *ya'aqov* because he cheated Esau inside his mother's womb! This tradition, preserved in the literary periphery, far from the Book of Genesis, is utterly different from that found in the Torah: cheating his brother inside their mother's womb is not the same as innocently holding onto a brother's heel. In the principal telling of a story, where all eyes gaze, much effort will have been made to present the "official" viewpoint, the doctrine that the writer wanted to instill in his readers, whereas on the periphery, more ancient traditions will often survive—traditions *against* which the center was aimed. Hosea's "marginal" tradition was well known; it was the popular tradition, and an allusion to it of several words was enough for the prophet's audience to identify and recall its details.

Is it possible for us to reconstruct the fuller tradition to which Hosea refers? The Bible's only other story about the birth of twins is that of Perez and Zerah, the sons of Jacob's son Judah. Perez and Zerah are born from Judah's relations with his daughter-in-law Tamar, who disguised herself as a prostitute (see Gen 38). The writer of that story was from the Kingdom of Ephraim, rival of the Kingdom of Judah, and he sought to cast aspersions onto Judah, founder of the tribe and kingdom that bore his name, and particularly onto Perez, progenitor of the Davidic dynasty (see Ruth 4:18–22). For this reason Genesis 38 relates how Perez stole his brother's birthright in the moments before they emerged from their mother's womb:

> When the time came for her to give birth, behold, there were twins in her womb! While she was in labor, one of them put out his hand, and the midwife tied a crimson thread on that hand, to signify: This one came out first. But just then he drew back his hand, and out came his brother; and she said, "What a breach you have breached [*paratsta . . . parets*] for yourself!" So he was named Perez [*perets*]. Afterward his brother came out, on whose hand was the crimson thread; he was named Zerah. (vv 27–30)

The author of Genesis 38 used the birth story to allude to David's having stolen the birthright—the kingship—from Saul and his descendants, in a like-father-like-son scenario.

The relationship between Perez and Zerah's birth and Jacob and Esau's is signaled by the singular phrase that appears in both—"behold, there were twins in her womb!" The exact nature of this relationship—the birth story of the second set of twins being taken from the rejected story of the former—can still be detected in the interpretation covertly given for Zerah's name. The root of *zerah* means "to shine," and the story relates it to the "crimson [thread]" (*shani*) that was tied to Zerah's hand. (Rashi explained it was "on account of the *shining* appearance of the crimson [thread].") But the name derivation also—and perhaps better—suits Edom (Esau's other name), since *Edom* has the same spelling as *'adom*, "red," that is, crimson (see, e.g., Isa 1:18). What's more, Zerah was also the name of an Edomite clan (Gen 36:17; 1 Chron 1:37).

Apparently, then, in the popular, orally transmitted version of Jacob and Esau's birth, the midwife tied a red thread to the hand of Esau-Edom, who was about to be born, but Jacob cheated and successfully pushed his way out first—as is now told about Perez.

We have reconstructed an ancient tradition about the birth of Jacob and Esau by using a story that was cast in its mold (our suspicions having been triggered by the allusion in Hosea). The ancient story about Jacob and Esau was silenced and changed almost beyond recognition, but it influenced Perez and Zerah's birth story, in which we still detect traces of the original tale about Jacob and Esau.

Though the authoritative story no longer blames Jacob with any act of deceit in his mother's womb, the biblical writers did not manage to banish the ancient tradition entirely and it continued to make its way, told and retold, for generations. The rejected tradition surfaced not only in Hosea but in the words of other prophets, too, who mined the Pentateuch's stories for meaningful material with which to educate their listeners. Those prophets blamed the people of Israel with deceitful behavior reminiscent of Jacob's. When a prophet cried out " . . . Though I know that you are treacherous, that you were called a rebel from the womb . . ." (Isa 48:8), he meant that Jacob's name and perfidious nature were decided by his iniquitous deeds in his mother's womb, when he rebelled against his brother's authority. The prophecy in Jeremiah 9:3–5, too, contains an echo of this ancient explanation of Jacob's name:

> ³Beware, every man of his friend!
>> Trust not even a brother!
> For every brother acts deceitfully [*'aqov ya'aqov*],
>> every friend is base in his dealings.
> ⁴One man cheats the other,
>> they will not speak truth;

They have trained their tongues to speak falsely,
    they wear themselves out working iniquity.
⁵You dwell in the midst of treachery,
    in their treachery they refuse to heed Me, declares the
LORD.

Jeremiah, wanting to illustrate the rampant depravity and deceit he observed among the people, called upon the memory of Jacob and Esau. Not only friends can't be trusted, he says: beware of even your brother!

Let us return to Genesis where, we now know, a tradition about a prebirth act of deviousness was replaced by a tamer one that admitted a struggle from which Esau emerged the winner, the firstborn of Isaac and Rebekah. With the installation of this more palatable tradition, the transfer of the firstborn rights from Esau to Jacob was deferred until the next scene in the patriarch's biography, to which we now turn.

The episode begins with the words "When the boys grew up" (25:27). As usual, the Bible skips the years between birth and early adulthood (cf. Gen 4:1–2, about Cain and Abel). To indicate their having reached adulthood the storyteller relies on distinguishing features that characterize the brothers' individual natures: "Esau became a skillful hunter, a man of the outdoors; but Jacob was a blameless man who stayed in camp" (v 27). The characterizations are formally symmetric, each consisting of three elements in which the first is the brother's name and the third his work-sphere: Esau the hunter is "a man of the outdoors," while Jacob "dwelled in tents," an allusion to his being a shepherd (cf. what was told of Jabal in Gen 4:20: "he was the ancestor of those who dwell in tents and amidst herds [lit., "tent and livestock dwellers"]"). No symmetry exists, however, between the central elements: Esau was "a skillful hunter," whereas Jacob was "blameless." This was noticed by the writer of the apocryphal Jubilees, a book written in the second century b.c.e. that retells the stories of Genesis and Exodus, who added a derogatory characteristic to Esau to balance the positive one given Jacob: "Jacob was a blameless and upright man while Esau was ruthless, a man of the field, and hairy; and Jacob stayed by the tents" (19:13).

This desire to grant Jacob a certificate of blamelessness should attract our attention. In a moment, the fateful story of the selling of the birthright—one of the two watershed scenes in Jacob's life—will commence. The narrator, it seems clear, is trying to erase any impression of Jacob as a cheater, and to prepare us to read the next story as he wants us to.

The asymmetry continues in the next verse:

Isaac loved Esau   because he had a taste for game,
But Rebekah loved Jacob   ———— (v 28)

This verse, too, prepares us for an approaching difficulty, in this case, the story of Jacob's stealing the blessing that Isaac intends for Esau, since it offers an explanation for Isaac's favoritism. The verse distinguishes between the two parents' love: the love of the mother is unconditional and unqualified, whereas Isaac's love hinges on corporeal matters—the food that Esau brings him. Isaac is a glutton, and Esau, too, as quickly becomes apparent: "Once when Jacob was cooking a stew, Esau came in from the field, exhausted. And Esau said to Jacob, 'Stuff me with that red stuff, for I am exhausted'" (vv 29–30). The boorish Esau returns from the field, from hunting, and he is *'ayef*, which means "exhausted" but also "thirsty" (e.g., Ps 63:2: " . . . as a parched and thirsty [*'ayef*] land that has no water"). He smells the aroma of his brother's cooking and wants to eat. We note, too, Esau's exact words: "Stuff me [*hal'iteni*] with that red stuff . . ." The root *l-'-t*, "stuff," is used only this one time in the Bible, though it will appear frequently in rabbinic literature where it always refers to the feeding of animals. Having Esau use the verb with regard to himself emphasizes his poor manners, if not his brutish nature. The way he stutteringly refers to the food—literally, "that red red stuff [*ha'adom ha'adom hazeh*]"— comprises one more interpretation of the name Edom, "which is why he was named Edom" (v 30), and links his name to his vulgarity: impatient and hungry, he doesn't care what it is that his brother has prepared, he only wants to put it into his mouth, quickly.

Both of these efforts of the writers have prepared us for Jacob's response to Esau's demand: "Jacob said, 'Sell now your birthright to me'" (v 31). We would have expected Jacob to try to alleviate his brother's distress quickly, to give him food and drink with no conditions and (it goes without question) no expectation of payment. Not only is this not the case, but Jacob demands the highest price—the birthright—for a simple bit of food. Isaac Abarbanel, the fifteenth-century Bible commentator, was astonished at Jacob's conduct:

> Had Jacob been blameless and upright, how could he have dared to tell his older brother to sell him his birthright for a bit of lentil porridge, since it is not worthy of a God-fearing man who turns from evil to covet something that is not his, all the more so buying from him the birthright for a contemptible price such as a bowl of lentil porridge. And if Esau is a foolish man, Jacob should have been a just man and not trick him . . .

Impulsive and reckless, Esau is untroubled by Jacob's outrageous demand. On the contrary, he is agreeable to the exchange: "I am at the point of death, so of what use is my birthright to me?" (v 32). Esau does not comprehend the birthright's significance and the far-reaching consequences for his descendants; he doesn't see beyond the present moment. A hunter who lived in constant danger of predatory beasts, certainly his own death could come at any moment and, anyway, the birthright would not bring him any immediate, physical satisfaction of the sort that he was used to enjoying.

In response, Jacob hurries to seal the deal, even demanding that his brother take an oath: "Swear to me first" (v 33). Esau, predictably, hesitates not a moment: "So he swore to him, and sold his birthright to Jacob." Now Jacob can afford to be generous, and he offers his brother even more than the promised porridge: "Jacob then gave Esau bread and lentil stew" (v 34).

A run of five verbs closes the story—"and he ate and drank and rose and departed and spurned, Esau, the birthright"— further proving Esau's earthly, bestial nature as a man who does not pause to consider his actions. Another fact is perhaps even more significant: had we thought that Esau's thirst and hunger were what propelled him to accept Jacob's conditions, the story's ending bears witness that even *after* his hunger and thirst were satisfied, he still spurned the birthright, making his unworthiness utterly clear.

Parallel forces are thus evident in the story that postponed the transfer of the birthright from the twins' birth to their adulthood. On one hand, Esau is portrayed as unfit for the birthright, a man who hardly appreciated or understood its significance, making it fitting that it should have fallen to his brother. The writer takes pains to improve our opinion of the brother who purchased the birthright, labeling him "blameless." One might even say that Jacob sought the birthright because he was aware of the oracle, "older younger shall serve" (25:23), and he acted only to hasten the fulfillment of God's promise. But this effort to help God in His plan is not necessarily praiseworthy, and here we find the opposing force at work in the story: though the exchange was legitimate, we do not forget how, fundamentally, Jacob's readiness to bargain with his brother—to exploit the latter's weakness—is not particularly flattering. And indeed, the day is not far when Jacob will pay dearly for the transaction.

We find an interesting echo of the porridge-for-birthright story in the history of Israel and Edom relations. Following the Israelites' wanderings in the wilderness and their arrival on the eastern bank of the Jordan River, on their way to the Promised Land, Moses dispatches messengers from Kadesh to the king of Edom. The initial part of Moses' request emphasizes the nations' familial relations: "Thus says your brother Israel . . ." (Num 20:14). This time, though, it is Jacob who needs his brother's benevolence when he asks for permission to cross through the other's territory (v 17), but the king of Edom refuses and threatens military action (v 18). Once again the Israelites try to cajole the king by offering to pay for any water they or their cattle might drink (v 19), but the request is denied, and the Edomite army sets out to protect their borders (vv 20–21).

In this episode Esau-Edom takes revenge: for Jacob's having demanded payment for satisfying his brother's desperate thirst, his request for drinking water is now refused, even for payment. Since, according to Genesis, the brothers made peace with one another after Jacob returned from Haran (we will get to this in chapter 6), it is clear that the writer of Numbers wanted to portray Edom negatively. Apparently, the story in Numbers reflects the enmity that existed between the two nations in the period in which it was written. In Moses' recounting of the story in Deuteronomy, it is specified that God had warned the Israelites to behave well toward "your brothers the descendants of Esau" (2:4): "What food you eat you shall obtain from them for money; even the water you drink you shall procure from them for money" (v 6). In the continuation and almost identical request made to King Sihon of Heshbon, we learn that the Edomites agreed to Israel's request and gave them food and water in return for payment (vv 28–29). According to Deuteronomy, which describes fondness toward Edom (see 23:8: "You shall not abhor an Edomite, for he is your brother"), the product of a period in which there were evidently friendly relations between the peoples, this episode closed, and balanced, the account that had been opened with the story of the birthright: Jacob sold the lentil stew to Esau; now Esau sells water and food to Jacob.

Let's turn to echoes of our story in prophetic literature. The delicate balance found between criticism of both seller and buyer is absent in the words of prophets who were active in the period from the destruction of Jerusalem and Judah and the nation's subsequent exile in 587/6 b.c.e. until after the return from Babylon, some seventy years later. These prophets interpreted the story according to the prevailing atmosphere of their times.

We know from Psalm 137 that the Edomites collaborated with the Babylonians in the invasion and defeat of Judah and Jerusalem and the destruction of the First Temple: "Remember, O Lord, against the Edomites the day of Jerusalem's fall; how they cried, 'Strip her, strip her to her very foundations!'" (v 7; see also Lam 4:21–22). The prophet Obadiah spoke about the Edomites and their betrayal—"When foreigners entered his gates and cast lots for Jerusalem, you were one of them" (Obad 1:11)—and he called to Edom, saying: "I will make you least among the nations, you shall be most despised" (v 2). With his use of the term "most" [me'od]—in which we find the same letters as in 'Edom, only rearranged—Obadiah indicates his opinion that the Edomites' status as *most despised* was a permanent attribute, tied to their very name.

The foremost prophet of the destruction of the First Temple and its aftermath was Jeremiah. In Jeremiah's prophecy about Edom we find incorporated verses from Obadiah's prophecy, including the verse just cited, though with a slight change: "For I will make you least among nations, despised among men" (49:15). The wordplay in Jeremiah, between *'adam* (men) and *'edom*, is more obvious than what we saw in Obadiah, between *me'od* and *'edom*. This prophecy deftly returns us to the pivotal stories of Jacob's early years and, in its condemnation of Edom, roundly attributes the young Esau's displacement to God: the words "I will make you *least* [*qaton*]" make it clear that God was responsible for reversing the order of the brothers, making Jacob—who is described as Rebekah's "younger [*qatan*] son" (Gen 27:42)—into the firstborn and Esau into the *qatan*. The word *bagoyim* ("among nations") returns us to the birth story and to the oracle's words that "two nations [*goyim*] are in your womb . . ." (25:23), to remind us that it was God's plan from the start that Esau would serve his brother, that "older younger shall serve." The word "despised" (*bazui*) relates to the end of the birthright episode, where we read that "Esau despised the birthright" (25:34): Esau despised the birthright, so it is only fitting that he should be despised!

Malachi, another prophet from the period of the Return from Exile, also expressed bitterness over the Edomites' participation in the First Temple's destruction. At the beginning of his prophecy he characterizes God's relations with the two nations Edom and Israel. In this prophecy we hear another echo of the stories that open the Jacob story cycle:

> I have shown you love, said the Lord. But you ask, "How have You shown us love?" After all—declares the Lord— Esau is Jacob's brother; yet I have loved Jacob and have hated Esau. I have made his hills a desolation, his territory a home for beasts of the desert. If Edom thinks, "Though crushed, we can build the ruins again," thus said the Lord of Hosts: They may build, but I will tear down. And so they shall be known as the region of wickedness, the people that the Lord has damned forever. Your eyes shall behold it, and you shall declare, "Great is the Lord beyond the borders of Israel!" (1:2–5)

While the beginning of the birthright story described how Rebekah loved Jacob (and Isaac loved Esau), in Malachi's prophecy it is God who loves Jacob and hates Esau, from which we realize that it was not Jacob's actions that precipitated his fate but God Himself.

2

"He should cheat me twice? He took my birthright
and now he has taken my blessing!":
Jacob the Deceiver

WITH THE taste of the birthright incident still bitter in our mouths, we find ourselves before yet another, even more difficult episode in which Jacob challenges the dominant position of his older twin. The story told in Genesis 27, where Jacob steals the blessing his father intended for Esau, is the direct continuation of the birthright purchase story. Its plotline is propelled by the father's love for his firstborn—rooted in Isaac's fondness for the meat that Esau feeds him—and the mother's unconditional love for the younger Jacob (25:28). The story opens with meetings between each pair of protagonists: the father and his favorite son, and the mother with hers.

It begins with a report of Isaac's advanced age and blindness (27:1), features that will soon play a key role. The elderly father, feeling his approaching death, asks to enjoy—perhaps for the last time—the mouthwatering meat that his son prepares so well: " . . . take your gear, your quiver and bow, and go out into the open and hunt me some game. Then prepare a dish for me such as I love . . ." (v 4). Isaac's use of the word "love" to indicate his fondness for the meat stew reminds us of another verse, "Isaac *loved* Esau because he had a taste for game" (25:28), and confirms the father's love for meat as critical to his love for Esau. Isaac's blessing is intended as reward for Esau's good work, " . . . so that my innermost being may bless you before I die" (27:4). The Hebrew *nafshi* is difficult to render in English. Often translated as "my soul," "my innermost being," or even simply as "I," the primary meaning of *nefesh* in biblical Hebrew is "throat" or "appetite" (see, e.g., Ps 107:8–9). The writer's use of it here, then, is particularly fitting: Isaac's innermost being is essentially his hunger, his *nefesh*, and, once sated, is what will bless the son who fills it.

Isaac's act reflects the conviction (shared by other participants in the story) that words and blessings contain power, and the impact of a blessing by an important person—including an elderly father on his deathbed—is considerable (see, e.g., Gen 49 [Jacob] and Deut 33 [Moses]). As readers we cannot help but be offended at Isaac's intention to determine the future of his sons and the nations that will issue from them in exchange for a mouthful of meat. Our annoyance may even awaken our sympathy—or at least mitigate our judgment—toward the opposing pair's decision to fight back.

Rebekah knows of her husband's plans—"Rebekah had been listening as Isaac spoke . . ." (v 5)—and she tells Jacob a brief version before instructing him with her own swiftly conceived plan: "Now, my son, listen to my voice, to what I command of you. Go to the flock and fetch me two choice kids that I may make of them a dish for your father that he likes. And you shall take it to your father and he shall eat, for which he may bless you before he dies" (vv 8–10). The words "listen to my voice, to what I command of you" transfer responsibility for the upcoming deception to Rebekah, effectively lightening the burden of guilt from Jacob's shoulders: he is a son who obeyed his mother, while "fetch me"—that is, "fetch *for my sake*"—also conveys the sense that Rebekah is concerned for herself, and her son only helps his mother realize her ambitions (like Esau, who helps his father satisfy his craving). The story therefore employs the mother as it did the father, to create extenuating circumstances that are already at work exonerating Jacob for the terrible act he is about to commit.

And still, notwithstanding the mother's initiative, the reader does not clear Jacob entirely of guilt. The son's reaction betrays neither shock nor moral outrage, his single worry being that he might be caught: "But my brother Esau is a hairy man and I am a smooth[-skinned] man. What if my father feels me, and I will be like a deceiver in his eyes and bring upon myself a curse and not a blessing" (vv 11–12). Esau's being *sa'ir*, "hairy," is the etymology of his other name, Seir, and was referred to already in the birth story, "a hairy mantle all over" (25:25). Now this plays a crucial role in the story since it is by touch that Isaac will identify the son for the blessing. The word Jacob uses to describe himself, "smooth" can also connote one whose lips are "smooth," that is, one who speaks falsely, a meaning found in Psalm 12:3: "Men speak lies to one another; their speech is *smooth*, they talk with duplicity." Jacob, in describing his physical appearance, simultaneously (and unintentionally) alludes to his inner nature. But Rebekah will not allow logic to interrupt her plan; she reassures Jacob that "Upon me your curse, my son," and immediately resumes her directions: "only listen to my voice. Go, fetch [them for] me" (v 13).

Rebekah leaves Jacob with no recourse. She is the active figure, he the passive one: "Rebekah took the clothes of Esau her older son, the finest that were with her in the house and she dressed Jacob her young son and the skins of the goat kids she dressed over his hands and on the smooth part of his neck" (vv 15–16). Jacob is referred to as "her young son," though we have just learned that he is already forty years old (Gen 26:34)! The image of a forty-year-old man standing, arms outstretched, waiting for his mother to dress him invites ridicule and wonder. Submissive obedience may be a tolerated excuse for a young boy who carries out his mother's morally questionable directions, but certainly not for a grown man.

As the text stands, Rebekah dresses Jacob in "clothes [that were] the finest [*bigdei ... hahamudot*]." Evidently, however, the original reading of the verse was *bigdei ... hahamutsot*, "clothes [that were] foul-smelling, reeking"—a change produced by the substitution of *d* for *ts*, phonemes commonly interchanged in the Bible. The reading makes sense: foul-smelling clothes will convince Isaac that Jacob is indeed his brother! When Isaac breathes in the sour smell of the blood-splattered clothes, he will have no doubt that Esau the hunter sits before him. The word *hamutsot* is another covert interpretation of Esau's other name, Edom, since *hamuts* also means '*adom*, "red."

Rebekah's chosen method for deceiving her husband— disguise—is found throughout literature, from the Bible to Shakespeare and Molière. The cunning stratagem is a literary convention that always works. But the moral principles that guide and shape the Bible require that, within its pages, impersonators will be made to pay for their deception. It's worth mentioning that, in Hebrew, a lexical connection exists between *beged*, "garment, [piece of] clothing," and *begidah*, "betrayal"; between *me'il*, "overcoat," and *me'ilah*, "treachery"; between *kesut*, "covering (such as a garment)," and *kisui*, "concealment," that is, hiding one's true intentions. Clothing facilitates deceit.

With Jacob wearing his brother's garments, Rebekah places the food she prepared into his hands and sends him off to his father. But for the fact that only one who is present to hear a blessing can be blessed by it, we begin to suspect that Rebekah would have taken Jacob's place and gone to Isaac herself.

Now, as the representatives from the two "couples" finally

meet, the story's tensions peak. To Isaac's question "Who are you, my son?" (v 18), Jacob hastily replies with a lie: "I am Esau, your first-born; I have done as you told me. Pray sit up and eat of my game, so that your soul/throat [*nafshekha*] may bless me" (v 19). Jacob's emphatic lie has caused centuries of readers extreme discomfort. It drove the writer of the Book of Jubilees to change Jacob's answer slightly: "I am your son. I have done according to your words" (26:13). The Rabbis, trying a different approach, divided Jacob's answer: "*I am* destined to receive the Ten Commandments, but Esau is *your firstborn*" (*Genesis Rabbah* 65:18). These solutions are not merely clever efforts to neutralize Jacob's blatant lie but reflect the belief that a divine plan was at work behind his actions. Another expression of this worldview is found in a midrash that explains how God even helped with the deception: "When Esau was hunting and tying [his catch], the angel was untying and setting it free. Again the angel would set it free. And why? In order to prolong the hours until Jacob will go and do [what he needs] and goes in to his father and his father will eat and Jacob will take the blessing" (*Tanḥuma Buber, Toledot* 10).

Back to the Bible. Isaac does not quite believe his ears and he asks, "How did you find it so quickly, my son?" (v 20). Jacob, knowing his father and his father's unfaltering faith in God, answers, "Because the Lord your God granted me good fortune." Perhaps Jacob refers to God as "the Lord your God" in an attempt to sound like the dismissive Esau: God is the God of Isaac, and not necessarily that of Esau. Isaac, however, is not so easily deceived. Blind, he turns to his sense of touch: "Come closer that I may feel you, my son—whether you are really my son Esau or not" (v 21). Once again, the midrash tried hard to redeem Jacob: "When Isaac told Jacob, 'Come closer that I may feel you, my son,' Jacob urinated onto his calves, and his heart became as soft as wax, and God assigned to him two angels, one on his right and one on his left, in order to hold him up by his elbows" (*Genesis Rabbah* 65:19). Be that as it may, the hairy mantle Jacob wears frustrates the old man's attempts, and he is confused. "The voice is Jacob's voice, yet the hands are Esau's hands" (v 22), he mumbles. At this point, the bewildered Isaac seems justified in blessing Jacob—"He did not recognize him, because his hands were like those of his brother Esau, hairy, and he blessed him" (v 23)—but at the very last moment he stops, and again wonders, "Are you really my son Esau?" Jacob responds unequivocally: "I am" (v 24).

With the mouthwatering aromas of the stew wafting into his nostrils, Isaac asks to eat, and again we are reminded of the relationship between the food that enters Isaac's mouth and the blessing that leaves it: "Serve me and let me eat of my son's game that my soul/throat may give you my blessing" (v 25). Note his specifying "my son's game," but not "my son Esau's game." The food and drink buy a bit more time, but at the meal's conclusion the moment of truth arrives. Isaac turns for help to one more sense, smell: "Then his father Isaac said to him, 'Come close and kiss me, my son'; and he approached and he kissed him. And he smelled his clothes and he blessed him" (vv 26–27). The sour smell of Esau's garments did the job, ostensibly assuaging any lingering doubts. It is with this same faculty, then, that Isaac begins his blessing: "Ah, the smell of my son is like the smell of the field that the Lord has blessed" (v 27); the blessing fits the hunter, the "man of the field" (25:27; 27:3).

The two-part blessing that Isaac now bestows on Jacob opens with an invocation of fruitfulness: "May God give you of the dew of heaven and the fat of the earth, abundance of new grain and wine" (v 28). The Creator of the heavens and earth is called upon to bless the son through both his heavens and his earth: the entire world will act with favor on the blessing's recipient. The second part no longer speaks of the son-recipient but of nations: "Let peoples serve you, and nations bow to you" (v 29). The nature of the relations that will prevail between the brothers was unmentioned, until now: "Be master over your brothers, and let your mother's sons bow to you." The repetition of the verb and object, "bow to you," indicates that what was stated initially in a general way applies, finally, to the relations between Jacob and Esau. The blessing supposedly presents the solution to the enigmatic oracle Rebekah received back in 25:23: "Two nations are in your womb, Two peoples shall issue from your loins; One people shall be mightier than the other, Older younger shall serve," but the explanation is still elusive, since the identity of the son being blessed remains hidden from Isaac.

Isaac is also unaware that, with the blessing's closing— "Cursed be they who curse you, Blessed be they who bless you"—which resembles the blessing God gave Abraham in Genesis 12:3, Isaac grants Jacob absolute protection from those who will want to curse him once his deception is discovered—first and foremost, Esau.

The events proceed quickly in a wondrous synchronization: "And it happened when Isaac had finished blessing Jacob, and Jacob had just left the presence of Isaac his father, that Esau came from his hunt" (v 30). Our relief is momentary, however, for we watch Esau, who has also prepared food for his father, and who now stands before him, unaware of the dramatic and fateful events that have unfolded in his absence. With this meeting, the second between the father and his favorite son, the drama reaches a crescendo. "Who are you?" (v 32) the bewildered father asks, to which Esau replies, "I am your son, your first-born Esau!" Esau's choice to identify himself as "first-born" makes us wonder: does he repress the fact that he already sold his birthright—his firstborn rights—to Jacob? Or perhaps he regrets having sold it, despite his having initially spurned it (25:34)?

The father is taken aback by the duplicate Esau: "Isaac was

seized with a great and violent trembling. 'Who was it then,' he demanded, 'that hunted game and brought it to me? I ate it all before you came and I blessed him; now he remains blessed!" (v 33). Spluttering out this long sentence, Isaac appears to slowly realize the deception and that the real Esau now stands before him. The clock cannot be turned back: blessings, once given, cannot be revoked.

Esau's shock is even greater than his father's, and his outburst is one of the purest, most heartbreakingly desperate in Genesis: "He burst into wild and bitter sobbing, and said to his father, 'Bless me too, Father!'" (v 34). It is for the stolen blessing that he cries—he does not care who took it from him. Isaac avoids answering whether he still has the power to bless Esau; instead, he identifies the deceiver: "Your brother came with deceit and took your blessing" (v 35). Isaac does not hesitate to call a spade a spade: Jacob deceived him.

Esau's reaction is twofold. "Was his name called Jacob that he should *cheat me* twice? He took my birthright and now he has taken my blessing!" (v 36). With this response Esau interprets Jacob's name as deriving from the root '-*k-b* (an interpretation, we recall, that was rejected in the birth story in favor of the milder etymology that related Jacob's name to his heel-holding [25:26]). This etymology, which speaks of a grave flaw in Jacob's character, was well known. It could not be entirely ignored, and so the storyteller chose to relieve the narrative pressure through a safety valve: he placed this condemnatory etymology into the mouth of one whose credibility we have come to doubt. How can Esau brazenly claim that Jacob cheated him of his birthright after he himself relinquished it, even swearing to Jacob beforehand? The narrator expects readers to dismiss Esau's words as incredible.

The despairing Esau again entreats his father: "Have you not reserved a blessing for me?" Isaac can no longer avoid responding and he answers rhetorically: "But I have made him

master over you: I have given him all his brothers for servants
and sustained him with grain and wine. What, then, can I still
do for you, my son?" (v 37). In this answer Isaac reverses the
order of the elements in the blessing, beginning with the relations between the brothers/nations since that is the element that
affects Esau most critically. Esau, for his part, is not deterred:
"Have you but one blessing, Father? Bless me, too, Father!"
(v 38) he weeps, bitterly. Moved, Isaac reconsiders and, finally,
blesses him:

> See, your abode shall be from the fat of the earth
> And from the dew of heaven above.
> Yet by your sword you shall live,
> And you shall serve your brother;
> But when you grow restive,
> You shall break his yoke from your neck. (vv 39–40)

The structure of Esau's blessing is similar to Jacob's: it
speaks first of the earth's fecundity and proceeds to a characterization of the relations between the brothers/nations. Nevertheless, the difference is conspicuous, most noticeably in the
blessing of fruitfulness: in Esau's blessing, God is not mentioned as the one who will bless him and give him "from the fat
of the earth and from the dew of heaven." Nor is Esau blessed
with "[an] abundance of new grain and wine," as was Jacob.
Readers mustn't assume that Isaac simply shortened the blessing and that he meant "Your abode shall be (blessed) from the
fat of the earth and (blessed) from the dew of heaven above,"
as in Moses' blessing of Joseph (Deut 33:13). Rather, a different meaning of the prefix *min* (which we have translated with
"from": "*from* the fat of the earth . . ." and "*from* the dew . . .")
must have been intended, like what is found in Micah 3:6:
"Therefore, night, for you, shall be *far from* prophesying, and
darkness, for you, shall be *far from* divination" (Micah speaks
angrily at false prophets, telling them: you will no longer have

visions at night, you will no longer be able to divine the future). Isaac's blessing of Esau therefore begins with ambiguity: Esau may believe that his father blesses him (and so the blow is softened) when, in fact, the blessing of the land belongs entirely to Jacob, and Esau shares no part in it, being *far from* it!

The notion that Esau will not share in the land's fruitfulness explains a further peculiarity, namely why, in the next verse, Isaac specifies that "by your sword you shall live": since Esau will not derive his living from the land, his sword will provide his livelihood. But even the strength of Esau's sword is restricted: "you shall serve your brother," making explicitly clear that this is not, in fact, a blessing. The news that he will serve his brother matches what was said in his brother's blessing—"Be master over your brothers, and let your mother's sons bow to you" (v 29)—and returns us to the oracle, "older younger shall serve" (25:23), which is now elucidated as meaning "the older shall serve the younger."

Isaac's final words, "But when you grow restive, you shall break his yoke from your neck," may actually be a later addition. I surmise this for two reasons. Whoever added them presumed that the blessing could not end without some sort of hope; and the addition makes the prophecy up-to-date, matching it to historical events that would occur—specifically, Edom's casting off Israel's yoke during the reign of King Joram (2 Kings 8:20) or King Ahaz (2 Kings 16:6).

Did Esau perceive just how inferior his blessing was and how it represented a type of consolation prize? In any event, he burned with murderous rage: "Now Esau harbored a grudge against Jacob because of the blessing which his father had given him, and Esau said to himself, 'Let but the mourning period of my father come, and I will kill my brother Jacob'" (v 41). The narrator seems to have dozed off for a moment when he wrote that Esau expressed his wrath "to himself" (lit., "in his heart"), since the very next verse states clearly that his words were reported to Rebekah and that "she sent for her younger son Jacob and said to him, 'Your brother Esau is consoling himself by planning to kill you'" (v 42).

Once again, Rebekah knows of plans that threaten Jacob. Before, she created the plot's complication; now she tries to resolve it. Again, her confidence in her plan is absolute. Using the exact same words, she commands Jacob's attention: "Now, my son, listen to my voice. Flee at once to Haran, to my brother Laban. Stay with him a few days, until your brother's rage subsides—until your brother's anger against you subsides—and he forgets what you have done to him. Then I shall fetch you from there. Let me not lose you both in one day!" (vv 43–45). Failure, as usual, is anonymous: Rebekah does not acknowledge that it is because of her that Esau now seeks murderous revenge on Jacob. She places the responsibility, instead, on Jacob: "and he forgets what *you* have done to him." Her egocentrism is also glaring: she does not bewail the notion that both her sons might die "in one day" (Jacob from Esau's hand and Esau by the hand of the blood-avenger) but mourns, "let me not lose you . . ."

Readers soon see that Rebekah will pay for her involvement in the events. In the previous chapter we saw how the oracle was added to the birth story at a secondary stage in order to extend partial justification to the mother's actions, to her efforts to accelerate the implementation of God's plan. But God, it turns out, neither wants nor needs help. On the contrary, he expects people to be patient and to prove their faith by waiting for His promises to be fulfilled. Rebekah was in a hurry to steer events, and her punishment is forthcoming.

Jacob's punishments are also forthcoming, some imminently, others in later chapters of his life. But while the sense that Jacob deserves punishment for his actions is undeniable, we also notice the extenuating circumstances that have been laid out in his defense: the father's conditional love for Esau and the mother's pressing and explicit demands that Jacob heed her. Also, the verses that envelop the story—the closing verses of chapter 26 and those that follow the story—represent a secondary layer added to lighten our impression of Jacob's unscrupulousness by emphasizing Esau's unworthiness. The ending of chapter 26 brings a quick report: "When Esau was forty years old, he took to wife Judith daughter of Beeri the Hittite, and Basemath daughter of Elon the Hittite; and they were a source of bitterness to Isaac and Rebekah" (vv 34–35). Taking Canaanite wives surely makes Esau unworthy of the blessing: we need only recall how, when it was time for Isaac to marry, a servant was sent to Haran, Abraham's homeland, to find a wife from their own people. Abraham had made his elderly servant swear "that you shall not take a wife for my son from the daughters of the Canaanites among whom I dwell" (24:3). Readers are thus surprised that, despite Esau's marriages, Isaac still wanted to bless him.

Immediately following Rebekah's directions to Jacob to flee for "a few days" come verses that converge with our knowledge of Esau's marriages to lend a more honorable character to Jacob's thievery and rushed departure, which was explained as an escape from his brother's wrath. Now, however, with Rebekah and Isaac taking the stage together for the first time in the story, the leave-taking is cast in different light. No longer a frenzied escape, it has become a journey with a destination: Rebekah complains to her husband, "I am disgusted with my life because of the Hittite women. If Jacob marries a Hittite woman like these from the daughters of the land, why do I live?" (27:46). Rebekah, who cried out during the pains of pregnancy, " . . . If so, why am I?" (25:22), now cries dramatically, "why do I live?" These words, too, will prove to be somewhat prophetic, as we will see.

In the meantime, Isaac takes heed of his wife's lament. He calls Jacob "and he blessed him and instructed him" (28:1). Isaac's readiness, his desire, really, to bless Jacob, now, indicates that the blessing he intended for Esau—which was taken by Jacob—was not his only blessing. It turns out that, all along, he had saved a blessing for his other son, Jacob. After giving the blessing, Isaac sends Jacob to Haran: "He instructed him, saying, 'You shall not take a wife from among the Canaanite women. Up, go to Paddan-Aram, to the house of Bethuel, your mother's father, and take a wife there from among the daughters of Laban, your mother's brother'" (28:1–2). The command includes one more blessing: "May El Shaddai bless you, make you fertile and numerous, so that you become an assembly of peoples. May He grant the blessing of Abraham to you and your offspring, that you may possess the land where you are sojourning, which God assigned to Abraham" (vv 3–4). Three times does some form of the word "bless" appear in these four verses, demonstrating not only that Isaac chose freely to bless Jacob but that to Jacob he gave the most valuable of all blessings, "the blessing of Abraham" for inheriting the land.

Jacob's dispatch to Haran makes obvious Esau's blunder in marrying the Hittite women: "And Esau saw that Isaac had blessed Jacob and sent him off to Paddan-Aram to take for himself a wife from there, blessing him, and that he had commanded him, saying, 'You shall not take a wife from among the Canaanite women,' and that Jacob had obeyed his father and mother and gone to Paddan-Aram" (vv 6–7; verse 6 contains another double appearance of the root "to bless"!). Jacob obeyed both his mother and father, his father's command having transformed his escape into an orderly departure for the purpose of finding a wife. Esau draws the obvious conclusion: "Esau realized that the Canaanite women displeased his father Isaac. So Esau went to Ishmael and took to wife, in addition to the wives he had, Mahalath the daughter of Ishmael, sister of Nebaioth" (vv 8–9). Esau's rage seems to have calmed, and his marriage to Mahalath seals the tale that began with his marriage to the Hittite women.

We note that Esau's taking a wife from Ishmael's daughters is no coincidence: he is the elder, rejected son, and he marries a woman from the house of another elder, rejected son: Ishmael, Isaac's older brother. Moreover, Esau's decision to marry, aimed at finding favor with his father, fails to achieve its aim—especially since Esau never divorces his Hittite wives. Esau's shame is undiminished and his disgrace endures.

Jacob's deceit, his having disguised himself in his brother's clothes, is alluded to—if obliquely—in the later prophecies. Before closing this chapter of Jacob's life, let's look at two of these prophecies, since they demonstrate the profound influence the story of Jacob's deception had for the biblical writers. First: the prophecy of revenge against Edom and the other nations that is found in Isaiah 63:1–6 (chapters 40–66 of Isaiah are not prophecies of the eighth-century b.c.e. prophet but the words of an anonymous prophet from the time of the Return to Zion). This prophecy is constructed on the foundations of the story of the robbing of the blessing:

[1]Who is this coming from Edom,
    in crimsoned garments from Bozrah;
Who is this, majestic in attire,
    pressing forward in His great might?
"It is I, who contend victoriously
    powerful to give triumph."
[2]Why is your attire so red
    your garments like his who treads grapes?
[3]"I trod out a vintage alone;
    of the peoples no man was with Me.
I trod them down in My anger
    trampled them in My rage;
Their life-blood bespattered My garments
    And all My clothing was stained.

⁴For a day of vengeance is my plan,
and My year of redemption arrived.
⁵Then I looked, but there was none to help;
I stared, but there was none to aid
So My own arm wrought the triumph
and My own rage was My aid.
⁶I trampled peoples in My anger
I made them drunk with My rage
And I will bring their glory to the ground."

Let's take a look at the parallels with our story. As is typical of biblical style, the writer uses an accumulation of similar words and expressions (though perhaps in different forms) in order to establish the connection between the two texts. These allusions were meant to alert us to a broader meaning.

a. In Genesis 27, Rebekah dresses Jacob in the clothes of Esau her older son, "the finest that were with her in the house" (v 15). The prophecy also focuses on clothing, on those worn by God when he returns from Edom in "crimsoned garments." In the story we find the verb *l-b-sh*, "wear," and the noun *b-g-d*, "garment, clothes"; in the prophecy we find two nouns for clothing, one derived from *l-b-sh* and one from *b-g-d*, each used twice: "in crimsoned *garments* [*begadim*] . . . majestic in attire [*bilvusho*]" (v 1); "Why is your attire [*lilvushekha*] so red, your garments [*uvgadeikha*] like his who treads grapes?" (v 2). As we've already discussed, in Genesis 27 two alternate readings are possible: *bigdei hahamudot* ("finest clothes") and *bigdei hahamutsot* ("crimsoned, foul-smelling clothes"). The prophecy uses the same word combination—*hamuts begadim*, "crimsoned, foul-smelling garments"—to describe God's clothes. The prophet alluded to the reading "finest clothes" when he depicted the clothing as "majestic in attire," but he also reads the expression as *hamuts:* God comes from Edom as a hunter returning from his kill, his clothes sour-smelling and red-stained with the blood of his victims. And, in perfect symmetry, Esau is described as having "*come* from his hunt" (27:30) as is God said to have "*come* from Edom" (Isa 63:1), from killing Esau's descendants.

b. Isaac blesses Esau: "But when you grow restive [*tarid*], you shall break his yoke . . ." (27:40). In the Septuagint the verse reads a bit differently: "and when you bring down [*torid*] and break his yoke . . . ," the version with which the prophet was evidently familiar. In the prophecy, God speaks of his anger toward Esau's descendants, "and I will bring their glory to the ground" (v 6), that is, he will destroy their hope.

c. About Esau is said: "and Esau said *to himself* [lit., "in his heart"], 'Let but the mourning period of my father come, and I will kill my brother Jacob" (27:41). God, seeking revenge on Edom, says: "For a day of vengeance is my plan [lit., "is in my heart"]" (63:4).

d. Rebekah tells Jacob, "Your brother Esau is consoling himself [*mitnahem*] by planning to kill you" (v 42). Finding the right English equivalent of *mitnahem* is problematic. While the root usually means "to console, comfort," in the reflexive form used here it can also, interestingly, mean "to (seek) revenge" (e.g., Isa 1:24). This, apparently, is the meaning of the verb here, too: "Your brother Esau is seeking revenge, to kill you." In Isaiah 63 God reveals his hidden plan: "a day of *vengeance* [*naqam*] is my plan" (v 4).

e. Rebekah hopes that Esau's anger will be forgotten: "until your brother's *rage* [*hemah*] subsides—until your brother's anger ['*af*] against you subsides" (vv 44–45). The same two terms, in reverse order, are used to describe God's anger against Edom: "I trod them down in My *anger* ['*api*], trampled them in My *rage* [*hamati*]" (v 3); "I trampled peoples in My *anger* ['*api*], I made them drunk with My *rage* [*hamati*]" (v 6).

Each of these parallels—and all of them together—set up an analogy between Esau and God: what is said in Genesis about Esau is said in the prophecy about God. The symmetry is significant: God will not forgive Esau/Edom for his desire to seek revenge against Jacob/Israel but instead will subject him to His own, corresponding rage. God will take revenge against Edom!

The story in Genesis was thus used as raw material by the prophet, who manipulated and interpreted it, removing it from its *peshat*, its plain meaning. At the same time, the hatred toward Edom that is expressed in the prophecy illuminates our story in new light. This prophetic reflection of the Genesis story presents Esau, who was there depicted as a blameless brother unknowingly deceived by both mother and brother, as a vengeance-seeker, as the evil brother deserving a measure-for-measure punishment.

Let's take a look at one more prophecy, the prophecy that begins the Book of Malachi, which we examined in the previous chapter.

> I have shown you love, said the Lord. But you ask, "How have You shown us love?" After all—declares the Lord— Esau is Jacob's brother; yet I have loved Jacob and have hated Esau. I have made his hills a desolation, his territory a home for beasts of the desert. If Edom thinks, "Though crushed, we can build the ruins again," thus said the Lord of Hosts: They may build, but I will tear down. And so they shall be known as the region of wickedness, the people that the Lord has damned forever. Your eyes shall behold it, and you shall declare, "Great is the Lord beyond the borders of Israel!" (1:2–5)

In Genesis Esau hates Jacob for his having stolen the blessing, "Now Esau harbored a grudge against Jacob . . ." (27:41), and in Malachi, God answers the one who plans vengeance, holding a grudge against Esau. While in Genesis Isaac thought it right to yield to Esau's pleas and give him a blessing that, at least ostensibly, bestowed fruitfulness on him (even if, as we remember, it was not really a blessing), the blessing does not commit God, who here curses Esau with a desolation that will never abate: "And so they shall be known as the region of wickedness, the people that the Lord has damned forever." This meaning of the verb z-ʿ-m—"to damn, to curse"—is known to us from Numbers 23:8: "How can I *damn* whom God has not *damned*?"

In Genesis we saw the beginning of a process of identifying meritorious facets of Jacob's behavior and blameworthy aspects of Esau's. Prophetic literature, we see, both continued and exaggerated that trend: with regard to the relations between the brothers/nations, Esau emerges as utterly wicked, Jacob as wholly virtuous. And now we return to Jacob, who has set out on his journey to Haran—whether to escape his brother's wrath or to find a wife and begin a family. He has been blessed twice, once through trickery, it is true, but the second blessing has reassured us of his chosen status. What his state of mind may have been, however, we can only wonder.

3

*"And behold, a stairway was set on the ground
and its head reached to the sky":
Jacob's Dream at Bethel*

PEOPLE CAN flee their pursuers while never breaking free
of their conscience and past. Jacob escaped his brother's wrath
but he left behind an elderly, blind father and a loving and wor-
ried mother without knowing whether he would see them ever
again. If he did turn to glance back, he caught a parting glimpse
of his country, the wide fields in which he had shepherded his
flocks and, stretched out above them, open sky. Who can know
his thoughts in those moments? Did he reflect on his behavior
toward his twin brother? Did he feel regret? The uncertainty
of his present journey into an unknown fate must have weighed
heavily on him. And into this mixture of thoughts and emotions, fear and possibly shame, perhaps the mission on which
his father sent him was beginning to stir some hope: hope of
finding a woman he would love and in whose arms he might
find comfort, a friend to confide in. It is not the way of biblical narrators to examine and reveal the thoughts and emotions

of their heroes. Instead, we are left to make do with what we have, with what they choose to narrate.

In the middle of nowhere, as a day of vigorous walking draws to a close, Jacob decides to pause before continuing his journey: "He came upon a place and stopped there for the night, for the sun had set" (Gen 28:11). This shepherd, accustomed to wandering after his flocks, is a homebody, a "tent dweller" and not a "man of the outdoors" (25:27) like his brother. Alone in the backcountry as the dark night cast its all-encompassing shadow, without his flock or sheepdogs to ease the loneliness, Jacob must suddenly have become singularly aware of his solitary predicament. He seems to have found little to comfort himself: "Taking one of the stones of that place, he put it under his head and lay down in that place" (v 11). Can it be that, in his rush, he hadn't stopped to gather even a single piece of clothing or blanket? He has brought nothing with which to cover himself or to put under his head and he uses a rock as a pillow, an apt illustration of his lonely circumstances.

Our hero lies on the cold, hard ground, gazing upward at the stars. It's late; he closes his eyes "and he dreamed" (v 12). Dreams have a prophetic quality in the Bible that allows one to peek behind the present-day and glimpse into the future. Actually, dreams represent one of the Bible's primary vehicles for prophecy, one of the principal mechanisms available to humans for communicating with God. We see this when Deuteronomy mentions—in one breath—"a prophet or a dream-diviner" (13:2), and King Saul realizes that God in His anger "did not answer him, either by dreams or by Urim or by prophets" (1 Sam 28:6). Will Jacob's dream reveal the future, only, or perhaps also something that has been concealed from us till now, his private reflections or something of his present circumstances?

Night closes around the sleeping Jacob but in his dream the stage is lit, earth and heaven both illuminated. It begins like a silent film that is gradually revealed in three stages, each opening with the words "And behold" (*vehinei*): "And behold, a stairway was set on the ground and its head reached to the sky" (v 12). This is the only occurrence in the Bible of the term *sulam*, here translated as "stairway," which we interpret by way of the Akkadian cognate *simmiltu*. It reminds us of the *ziggurat*, the stepped tower-temples of Mesopotamia that served as a link between the gods in the heavens and humankind on earth. In a moment we will look carefully at the distinct context that Babylonian literature provides for Jacob's dream, and its implications. We don't know who placed the stairway there, but the dreamer first perceives its foundations on the earth, where he is, and only afterward does his gaze rise to find its top in the sky. We notice the connection that is established between the rock that was placed "under his *head*" and the stairway, with its "head" in the heavens.

The second stage: "And behold, angels of God were ascending and descending on it." First they ascend from the lower position of the dreamer; afterward they descend, from the top. They continue this ascending and descending, establishing an unceasing connection between upper and lower spheres. The angels provide company for Jacob; no longer is he alone.

A clear counterpart to the image of God's angels ascending and descending is found in the Babylonian myth "Nergal and Ereshkigal" in which gods are described using the staircase that connects the heavens with the netherworld. The biblical staircase connects heaven and earth, without extending to the netherworld, to Sheol. Such an extension would not serve the dream or its message, and would not have sat easily with the biblical worldview, which is not entirely comfortable with the notion of an afterlife in Sheol.

In the dream's third stage, Jacob finally dares to look to the top of the staircase, to the heavens: "And behold, God was standing on it" (v 13). The angels created the first connection

between heaven and earth; now God's voice reaches down to
Jacob, and the silence is broken. God introduces himself, "I
am the Lord, the God of your father Abraham and the God
of Isaac," reassuring Jacob that the God of Abraham and Isaac
is still also his God, even now. Moreover, prior to his leaving
the Land of Canaan, his father had blessed him with the blessing that God would grant him "the blessing of Abraham," the
blessing of inheriting the land (28:4). Now he receives confirmation that he (and not his brother) is the one chosen to
continue the genealogy, and that he will inherit the land: "the
land on which you are lying I will assign to you and to your offspring" (28:13). Actual circumstances penetrate into the dream
as God reminds Jacob that he lies on the earth—symbolizing
how the land will become his—and that his separation from it
will be temporary. God also refers to Jacob's descendants, con-
firming the success of his present journey: "Your seed shall be
as the dust of the earth; you shall spread out to the west and to
the east, to the north and to the south" (v 14).

Whereas a moment previously Jacob's world had suddenly been compressed by an all-encompassing darkness closing
around his weary body, a vast world has now opened before him.
Three axes become apparent: the vertical connection between
earth and heaven; the horizontal dissemination of Jacob's descendants in all four directions; and a temporal line embracing
both past and future, reaching from Abraham and Isaac to Jacob
and the generations that will issue from him. God's promise to
Jacob indeed contains an echo of the earlier promise made to
Abraham, after Abraham parted from his brother's son (just as
Jacob is now given the promise after leaving his brother): "And
the Lord said to Abram . . . 'Raise your eyes and look out from
where you are, to the north and south, to the east and west,
for I give all the land that you see to you and your offspring
forever. I will make your offspring as the dust of the earth, so
that if one can count the dust of the earth, then your offspring

too can be counted'" (13:14–16). The continuation of Jacob's blessing, "All the families of the earth shall bless themselves by you and your seed" (v 14), further reminds us of God's blessing to Abraham, which accompanied the divine command to "Go forth from your land and from your birthplace and from your father's house to the land that I will show you . . . all the families of the earth shall bless themselves by you" (12:1, 3) and was given in a similar context. Even though Jacob walks in the opposite direction, from the Promised Land back to the land of his grandfather's birth, it is precisely at this point, as he leaves the Land of Canaan, that he needs a blessing that will promise his return.

But promises for the future are not enough: Jacob urgently needs support now. He needs protection, knowledge that he is not alone on his journey into the unknown. And, truly, his fortification is not long in coming: "And behold, I am with you; I will protect you wherever you go and will return you to this land. I will not leave you until I have done what I have promised you" (v 15). Does the vertical movement of the angels symbolize Jacob's movement to Haran and back, even giving material expression to God's protection? This was the conclusion of the Rabbis, who distinguished between two groups of angels, those who ascended and those who descended: "angels that accompany man in the land (of Israel) do not accompany him outside the land (of Israel), the ones who ascend are those that accompanied him in the land of Israel; those who descend accompanied him outside the land" (*Genesis Rabbah* 68:12).

Flustered and excited by what he has seen and heard, Jacob wakes, though it is still night: "Jacob awoke from his sleep and said, 'Surely the Lord is present in this place, and I did not know it!'" (v 16). Now he understands that the place in which night overtook him was not just *any* place, but is holy, a place in which God is present. The reader, too, understands now what the narrator implied at the very beginning of the episode: " . . . He came upon *the* place and stopped there" (v 11). The Hebrew text, originally unvocalized, can reflect either "a place" (*bemaqom*) or "the place" (*bamaqom*). At this point we realize that it should be read with the definite article: Jacob stopped at *the place*, a certain place that is a sacred site, as conveyed by the word *maqom* in other verses (e.g., Gen 12:6 and cf. Arabic *maqam*).

On the heels of his new awareness comes fear: "And he was afraid, and said: 'How awesome is this place! This is none other than the house of God, and this is the gateway to heaven'" (v 17). A meeting with God, with the Sacred, along with God's comforting words, is enough to make anyone faint, all the more so in the darkest hours of the night. Yet despite his fears, Jacob now apprehends something else: the place in which he has met God is special. It is God's abode, His heavenly home: there and only there is the gate of heaven from which the staircase descends earthward and connects the heavenly and terrestrial realms.

Did Jacob fall back asleep once the vision was over? Or perhaps the powerful experience and the auspicious tidings he received left him awake, full of thoughts, until dawn? The narrator tells nothing except that, when light does arrive, Jacob acts with purpose: "And Jacob rose early in the morning and he took the stone that he had put under his head and set it up as a pillar and poured oil on its head" (v 18). Jacob's act conveys both his belief in the sacredness of the place and his gratitude: notice the similarities between the verse about the stairway, "a stairway was set [*mutsav*] on the ground and its head reached to the sky," and what is written now, about the stone: " . . . that he had put under his head and set it up as a pillar [*matsevah*] and poured oil on its head." The pillar, the stone that Jacob now erects in a vertical position, is a cultic object that resembles the staircase Jacob saw in his dream. The oil he pours over it is a thanksgiving offering that sanctifies it. (Such pillars were later identified with idolatry and forbidden [Deut 16:21–22].)

The pillar's dedication is followed by Jacob's naming of the place: "He named that site Bethel [*beit 'el*, "house of God"]; but previously the name of the city had been Luz" (v 19). We now realize that Jacob's previous exclamation, " . . . none other than the *house of God* [*beit 'elohim*] . . ." (v 17), contained an etymology of the place-name.

Ancient Near Eastern sources know of a god named Bethel: a contract between Esarhaddon, king of Assyria, and the king of Tyre refers to this god, and in the city of Dura-Europos, in Syria, a dedicatory inscription was found, in Greek, to Zeus Bethel. In fact, the god Bethel is familiar to us even from the Bible: later, in exile in the house of Laban, Jacob will dream another dream in which God reveals himself: "I am the God Beth-el [*ha'el beit 'el*], where you anointed a pillar and where you made a vow to Me . . ." (31:13). Afterward, on his return from exile, Jacob will build an altar here and call the place El-bethel, "the god of Bethel" (35:7). The prophet Jeremiah leaves no room for doubt about the existence of such a god when he says: "And Moab shall be shamed because of Chemosh [the god of Moab], as the House of Israel were shamed because of Bethel, on whom they relied" (48:13).

Jacob makes a vow that expresses his expectation that God's promises will be fulfilled and that God will protect him from all evil (see above, v 15). He does not refer to the larger matters included in God's promises, regarding land and plentiful descendants. His thoughts are firmly in the present, on the challenges he must face in order to survive the present journey: "If God is with me and protects me on this way that I go, and gives me bread to eat and clothing to wear, and I return safely to my father's house, and the Lord will be my God. And this stone, which I have set up as a pillar, will be the house of God, and of all that You give me, I will set aside a tithe for You" (vv 20–22).

It is worth comparing God's promise to Jacob with Jacob's expectations:

Promise	Vow
[15]Behold, I am with you	[20]If God is with me
I will protect you wherever you go	and protects me on this way that I go
	and gives me bread to eat and clothing to wear
And will return you to this land . . .	[21]and I return safely to my father's house . . .

Whereas God promises protection on *all* of Jacob's future paths, Jacob thinks only of the present path. And to God's promise Jacob adds the most fundamental necessities, "bread to eat and clothing to wear." Of course, Jacob's specific mention of food and clothing reminds us of the two acts that awakened his brother's fury: his purchase of the birthright with food and his securing the blessing using his brother's clothing. Does Jacob also think of these previous acts as he makes his vow? Interestingly, while God promises to return Jacob "to this land," the Promised Land, Jacob's wish is to return home, "safely to my father's house."

The phrase at the very end of verse 21, "and the Lord will be my God," is not easily understood. Is it the conclusion to the protasis—one more "if," one more condition? Or is it the beginning of the apodosis, one of the consequences of Jacob's conditional vow, that is, "then the Lord shall be my God"? If the former, then Jacob means to say that God's fulfillment of His promises will include God's choosing to be Jacob's God and protector. The second possibility would portray Jacob at his most impudent: Jacob announces to God that he will adopt Him as his God only if God keeps His promises. The matter is left ambiguous.

Verse 22 returns us to the rock Jacob erected and anointed: "And this stone, which I have set up as a pillar, will be the house of God . . ." If God's promises are fulfilled, the pillar will be but the first act: Jacob promises that the stone "will be the house of God, and of all that You give me, I will set aside a tithe for You."

This story is a founding myth of the temple that was built in Bethel and became the primary temple in the Kingdom of Israel, the northern kingdom. It was the temple referred to in Amos as "a royal temple and House of the Kingdom" (7:13). The temple would be forever linked with the patriarch Jacob, who saw a wondrous vision at "this place": of the opening of heaven's gate, of God and His angels revealed, and of the promise of divine favor.

Until now we've interpreted the story of Jacob's dream at Bethel as an isolated tradition. I've already mentioned, however, that the story preserves memories of more ancient Babylonian traditions. Tracing those traditions reveals another dimension of Jacob's dream and contrasts Bethel to Babylon. Let us look at the story of the Tower of Babel in Genesis 11:1–9, a tale of unbounded human hubris. Humankind sought to build a tower that would reach the heavens in order "to make a name for ourselves" (v 4), to cross the boundary that separates humans from God. The humans fail completely, however, and their punishment comes swiftly: God disrupts their unity, scatters them over the entire earth, and even causes them to speak distinct languages, making communication between them impossible. The story concludes with an etymology of Babel, the site of their efforts to climb to heaven, deriving it from *balal*, "confuse, confound": "That is why it was called Babel, because there the Lord *confounded* the speech of the whole earth, and from there the Lord scattered them over the face of the whole earth" (v 9).

This etymology of *Babel* from *balal* was evidently an attempt to negotiate a more commonly known, Babylonian folk-etymology of the name: *Bab ili*, "Gate of the Gods," an interpretation known in Israel, as we will soon see. In fact, the entire story of the Tower of Babel polemicizes against this Babylonian conception that the temple-tower in Babylon, which was dedicated to the god Marduk, the head of the Babylonian pantheon, embodied a tribute to that god and the belief that Babylon was the place in which the earth and the heavens connected. According to Babylonian belief, the temple-tower in Babylon contained the gate to heaven. The Temple of Marduk in Babylon was called E-sag-ila, "The House of the Raised Head," and inside its compound rose the tower Etemen-an-ki, "The Foundation of Heaven and Earth." The description of Esagila's construction in the Babylonian creation epic "Enuma Elish" can still be heard in the biblical story of the Tower of Babel, where we read "Come, let us make bricks . . . Come, let us build us a city, and a tower with its head in the sky" (vv 3–4). In the Babylonian story we find:

> For one whole year they molded bricks.
> When the second year arrived,
> They raised high the head of Esagila equaling Apsu.
> Having built a stage-tower as high as Apsu.

> (tablet 6, lines 60–62; The Akkadian term *apsu*, which can
> be translated as something like "the freshwater deep,"
> referred to the vast waters in the underground aquifers, the
> meaning here being that the tower was as high in the sky as
> the waters were deep.)

The biblical writers, unwilling to accept Babylon—a city of idol-worshipers—as heaven's gate, found various ways to challenge the popular Babylonian tradition, and they presented the story of the tower's construction indirectly, as though through distorting mirrors, as a story of failure and human conceit. At the same time, they offered an alternative story that located the gate of heaven in the Land of Israel, the seat of the belief in one God. Their alternative story is the story of Jacob's dream in Genesis 28.

A close look and comparison of the stories of the Tower of Babel and Jacob's dream reveals the latter, the foundation myth of the cult at Bethel, to be the inversion of the Babel story. The building of the tower with its "head in the heavens" was a wrongheaded human initiative that ended in failure, while the vision of the stairway in Jacob's dream, with its "head" in the sky, is the manifestation of God's will. In the tower story, humanity sought to climb to heaven; in the story of the stairway, Jacob remains firmly on the ground while God's angels ascend and descend, spinning the connection between the heavenly and earthly realms.

God's position in the two stories is also contrasted. In order to observe the builders of the tower and punish them, God descends from His place: "The LORD came down to look at the city and tower that man had built" (11:5). But when God addresses Jacob, speaking words of promise and redemption, He remains on high, at the top of the stairway (28:13).

The builders of the city and tower in Babylon use bricks— "Brick served them as stone" (v 3)—perhaps an expression of astonishment, even mockery toward those who place their trust in man-made building blocks. Jacob, for his part, places a stone at Bethel (28:18), which becomes the foundation for God's abode: "And this stone, which I have set up as a pillar, will be the house of God" (v 22). The work of the tower-builders was antagonistic toward God; Jacob's positioning of the stone, and the construction of the House of the Lord on the same spot, were acts that promoted God's glory.

The builders of the tower initiated their project after they "migrated from the east" (11:2). Jacob leaves for "the land of the Easterners" (29:1) after he vows to erect a House of God on his safe return to his father's home in Bethel.

What's more, the tower-builders' fear "else we shall be scattered all over the world" is realized in their punishment (11:8–9), while to Jacob God promises the opposite, that he will be returned to his starting point: "and [I] will return you to this land" (28:15), a promise that will be fulfilled in later chapters of Jacob's story. In contrast to God's scattering the people "over the face of the whole earth" (11:8), God promises Jacob that he will "spread out to the west and to the east, to the north and to the south" (28:14): Jacob's descendants will fill the land. The story of the tower ends with a curse that essentially divides the people of the earth, while the climax of the story of the stairway is a unifying blessing: "All the families of the earth shall bless themselves by you and your seed" (28:14).

Finally, while both stories contain name derivations, the negative etymology given Babel, "confound," which reflects God's curse, is in stark contrast to the etymology given Bethel, which expresses God's presence there and promises blessing and hope: "And he was afraid, and said: 'How awesome is this place! This is none other than the house of God [*beit 'elohim*], and this is the gateway to heaven' . . . He named that site Bethel . . . and this stone, which I have set up as a pillar, will be the house of God [*beit 'elohim*]" (28:17, 19, 22). Jacob's words, "this is the gateway to heaven," are thus a polemic against those who located heaven's gate in Babylon, and proclaim its location in the temple in Bethel instead.

The transfer of heaven's gate from Babylon to Bethel, in which God Himself shows Jacob the gate's location, was not, however, its final stop. Bethel's prominence waned following the Assyrian conquest of the Kingdom of Israel and the destruction and defilement of its temple by King Josiah of Judah. The Judahite king destroyed Bethel and all other temples in Israel as part of his centralization of the cult (see 2 Kings 23:15–18). His revolution delegitimized all temples in the land except for the one in Jerusalem, in Judah, which became the single sanctioned place for worship. As a consequence, it became necessary to transfer the tradition about heaven's gate there, to Jerusalem.

This relocation is reflected in one of the versions of the story of the sanctification of Jerusalem in the days of David (2 Sam 24; 1 Chron 21). According to this episode, God punished the people by sending a destroying angel with a devastating plague over the land and then stopped it when it reached Jerusalem. God commanded David to erect an altar at the very place where the plague was arrested. The later version of the story in 1 Chronicles was written after Josiah's reform, even after the Babylonian exile, during the period of the Return to Zion. In this version we find that a verse has been added, "This will be the House of the Lord God and this the altar of burnt offerings for Israel" (22:1). The verse is written such that it superimposes itself onto verse 17 in Genesis 28. Compare "*This* is none other than the *house of God*, and *this* is the gateway to heaven" with "*This* will be the *House of* the Lord *God* and *this* the altar of burnt offerings for Israel." David's *altar of burnt offerings* will now, according to the author of this verse, provide the earth's connection with the Divine. Jerusalem, like Bethel previously, is fear-inspiring: like Jacob who, following the vision of divine beings, gasped, "How awesome is this place," so we now read how a vision of God's angel inspired David's fear in Jerusalem: " . . . he was terrified by the sword of the angel of the Lord." Within the verse in 1 Chronicles, we still hear echoes of the name-etymology for Bethel ("House of God"), which has now become the "House of the Lord God," intimating that Bethel is, in fact, but another name for Jerusalem, that Jerusalem is another name for Bethel. In Jerusalem, the connection between heaven and earth was now formed not by a stairway but by fire descending from heaven to the altar: "[David] invoked the LORD, who answered him with fire from heaven on the altar of burnt offerings" (21:26). Here it was not the stone, the pillar, that commemorated the connection, but the altar; it was not Jacob who stood at the crucial juncture between earth and heaven, but David, the Judahite founder of Jerusalem, and the sacrifices offered in Jerusalem were what marked it.

Chronicles' covert identification of Bethel with Jerusalem became overt in rabbinic literature, which returned to Jacob and his dream for explication:

> Jacob was seventy-seven years old when he went forth from his father's house . . . From Beer-Sheba as far as Mount Moriah [that is, the Temple Mount in Jerusalem] is a journey of two days, and he arrived there at midday . . . and stopped there all night, "for the sun had set" (Gen 28:11). Jacob took twelve stones of the stones of the altar, whereon his father Isaac was bound, and he set them for his pillow in the same place, to signify that there will descend from him twelve tribes, and all became one stone, to signify that all would be a great nation in the Land, as it is said, "And who is like Your people Israel, a unique nation on earth" (1 Chron 17:21) . . . And he was afraid and said, "How awesome is this place." . . . And Jacob returned to gather the stones, and he found them all [turned into] one stone, and he set it up for a pillar in the midst of the place. And oil came down for him from heaven, and he poured it on it, as it is said, "and he poured oil on its head" (v 18). What did the Holy One, blessed be He, do? He placed [thereon] His right foot, and sank the stone to the bottom of the depths, and He made it the keystone of the earth . . . for there is the navel of the earth, and there from was all the earth evolved, and upon it the Sanctuary of God stands, as it is said, "And this stone, which I have set up for a pillar, shall be God's house" (v 22). (*Pirkei de-Rabbi Eliezer* 35)

When those who had been exiled from Judah finally returned, in the period of the Return to Zion, they took it upon themselves to rebuild the temple. The Samaritans, who lived in northern Israel and saw themselves as the remnants of the Kingdom of Israel who had never left, wanted to join the construction effort but their offer was rejected. The anti-Samaritan agenda of Ezra 4, which calls the Samaritans the "adversaries of Judah and Benjamin" (v 1), is obvious. The chapter depicts the Samaritans as speaking words that contradict the Samaritan belief that they were Israelites who were not expelled by the Assyrians to Babylon, portraying them instead as new arrivals to the land: "Let us build with you," they are quoted as saying, "since we too worship your God, having offered sacrifices to Him since the time of King Esarhaddon of Assyria, who brought us here" (v 2; cf. 2 Kings 17:24–33). The response of the Judahite leaders is definitive: "It is not for you and us to build a House to our God, but we alone . . ." (v 3). Left with no alternative, the spurned Samaritans sanctified Shechem as the single place for worshiping God, and consequently identified Bethel not with Jerusalem but with Shechem. Shechem has thirteen names in Samaritan tradition, among them Luz, Bethel's previous name, and Bethel.

Thus, even when Bethel was rejected, the story of Jacob's stairway was not abandoned. Bethel wandered between Jerusalem and Shechem, though the story of Jacob and his dream remains fixed.

4

"It is not the practice in our place": Wives and Sons, A Mixed Blessing

THE BOOK of Genesis, steadfast in the ways of the biblical narrative, spends no time describing the hardships Jacob suffers on his journey from Bethel to Haran nor, as I've already mentioned, does it reveal any regrets he may have felt during the days and nights of his journey: Was his conscience bothered? Was he thinking of what might await him, at his uncle's house? The writer is silent; instead, all the days of journey have been condensed into a single verse, "Jacob resumed his journey and came to the land of the Easterners" (29:1), after which we find our protagonist already in Haran, standing by "a well in the field" (v 2). Had Jacob's parents ever told him about that other encounter beside a well in Haran, when God had revealed Rebekah to the servant Abraham had sent to fetch a wife for his son? We, in any event, know of that fateful meeting and now wonder whether this journey, which has led Jacob to a well in Haran, will also be the beginning of a love story and marriage.

The picture of the well encourages us to think just that. Shepherds whom Jacob chances upon answer favorably when asked whether they know his uncle Laban, and even point to Laban's daughter who now approaches, a sort of deus ex machina: "and there is his daughter Rachel, coming with the flock" (v 6). The image of his approaching cousin rouses Jacob's courage and strength and he manages to roll a large stone off the mouth of the well, a feat that usually requires the combined strength of a number of men. The adrenalized suitor hurries to water the young woman's flocks, perhaps in order to occupy himself until he can regain control over his pulsing excitement, but it fails in its objective and he rushes to Rachel—whose name means "ewe"—and kisses her. (We can't help but notice the wordplay between *vayashq*, "he watered," and *vayishaq*, "he kissed.") Jacob's tears—of happiness, to be sure, but also, we imagine, of release from the tensions of the last days—seal the encounter and Rachel hastens to tell her father. Only we know how the warm welcome Jacob receives from Laban hides the storm clouds that swell nearby.

After Jacob has spent a month in his uncle's home, Laban asks, "what will your wages be?" (v 15). Before conveying Jacob's answer, the biblical narrator relates a number of details about Laban's family that hint at an approaching complication: "Laban had two daughters; the name of the older one was Leah, and the name of the younger was Rachel. Leah had soft eyes; Rachel was shapely and beautiful" (vv 16–17). Though the exact meaning of the Hebrew adjective *rakh*, which usually means "soft," is not entirely apparent in that it is used here to describe Leah's eyes (are they weak? lusterless?), it clearly does not flatter Leah, and it is equally clear that her sister is the more beautiful one whom Jacob desires. In what appears to be a case of love at first sight, Rebekah's younger son has fallen in love with her brother's younger daughter, and the infatuated man proceeds to offer his services in exchange for the woman:

"I will serve you seven years for your younger daughter Rachel" (v 18). The fugitive Jacob, who recently arrived empty-handed in Haran, is able to supply the bride price only by his own labor; his abundant love for Rachel is expressed by the prolonged period—seven years—that he is willing to work in order to marry her. Laban's immediate consent—"Better that I give her to you than that I should give her to an outsider. Stay with me" (v 19)—betrays little joy on his part at the possible union, though neither does it warn of the deceit he will enact.

Seven years pass in Laban's service but to Jacob they feel "but a few days because of his love for her" (v 20). The irony in the narrator's word choice is stark: it was this exact expression, "a few days," that his mother had used when she sent him to Haran: " . . . Flee at once to Haran, to my brother Laban. Stay with him *a few days*, until your brother's rage subsides" (27:43–44). Rebekah's few days have stretched into years—she will never see her son again—while for the lovesick Jacob the years seem to have passed "like days" in his uncle's house.

Jacob finally demands his wages: "Give me my wife, for my time is fulfilled, that I may come to her" (v 21). This young man, itching to have relations with his long-desired Rachel, calls her "my wife" without mentioning her name, another allusion to what awaits: a woman will be given him, though it will not be Rachel. But let us not get ahead of ourselves. Laban carries on as expected, inviting the townspeople to the wedding feast. Under cover of darkness, however, he switches Rachel with Leah, his firstborn, whom no man seems interested in marrying because of some defect of her eyes. Only at dawn does the dismayed Jacob discover with whom he has shared the night, whom it is he has married. The duped newlywed is quick to protest to his father-in-law: "What is this you have done to me? I was in your service for Rachel! Why did you deceive me?" (v 25). Is it possible that Jacob said nothing to Leah when he discovered the ruse? Did he not accuse her of complicity in her father's deceit? And what about Rachel? She was equally complicit in the scheme, allowing the ruse to proceed and Jacob to be trapped. At the very least she understood that something was amiss when her father prevented her from entering Jacob's bed. The storyteller, however, does not give us a moment to reflect as he rushes to relate Laban's complacent retort to Jacob's angry bewilderment: "It is not the practice in our place to marry off the younger before the older. Wait until the bridal week of this one is over and we will give you that one too, provided you serve me another seven years" (vv 26–27). The time has finally come for Jacob to pay for having stolen his brother's blessing: "in our place"—Laban pronounces— matters are not conducted as they are in Canaan, where a younger sibling can bypass the firstborn and steal his rights. In Haran, a civilized society, he insinuates, the firstborn must be given firstborn rights. Laban indeed cheats Jacob, but how can the scheming Jacob protest, Jacob whom his own father has described as having "[come] with deceit and [taken] your blessing" (27:35)? The perceptive reader understands that Laban administers a measure-for-measure penalty on Jacob, and the perfectly mirrored symmetry between the two episodes seals the case: in the story of the stealing of the blessing, the mother, Rebekah, took advantage of the father's blindness to replace her firstborn son with the younger one. In the parallel episode, the father, Laban (who is Rebekah's brother), takes advantage of darkness (which prevents Jacob from seeing the bride's identity) to substitute his younger daughter with the firstborn.

The Rabbis noted the correspondence between the two stories and the punishment it signifies for Jacob. Their version answers a question we raised about Leah's participation in the ruse, as well.

> The entire night she pretended to be Rachel; he cried out to her, "Rachel," and she answered him. In the morning,

"there was Leah!" He told her, "You are a lying daughter of a liar! During the night did I not call out 'Rachel' and you answered me?" She said to him, "Is there a school without students? Did not your father call out to you, 'Esau,' and you answered him?" (*Genesis Rabbah* 70:17)

Let's return to Laban's reply to Jacob, specifically to the second part, "Wait until the bridal week of this one is over and we will give you that one too, provided you serve me another seven years" (v 27). Laban's trickery stemmed not only from his concern that his firstborn daughter find a husband but from a selfish greed that didn't allow him to pass up a chance to exploit Jacob, the devoted servant—if not slave—and subjugate him for another seven years of labor. Jacob's response is not even conveyed. What else could he do? His love for Rachel propels him to swallow his pride. Readers can only imagine what he felt, what he said to himself over the six remaining days of the wedding feast as he had to play the eager groom while silently preparing himself for an added seven years of service to Laban, his uncle and now father-in-law, who had cheated him.

As recorded in Genesis, the two marriage ceremonies follow one another in quick succession. Wedding follows wedding— but Jacob's affection toward his second wife, of course, is poles apart from what he feels toward Leah: "he cohabited with Rachel, too; indeed, he loved Rachel more than Leah" (v 30).

Finding himself as the husband to two women was therefore a direct result of the sin Jacob committed toward his father and brother; God on High makes certain to balance the books regarding every transgression, without exceptions. And if two wives were not enough, upon marriage each daughter receives a maidservant from her father (a custom known from extant Hurrian documents, the society of which Haran was a part). Both comments about the maidservants interrupt the natural rhythm of the story: "Laban had given his maidservant Zilpah to his daughter Leah as her maid" (v 24); "Laban had given his maidservant Bilhah to his daughter Rachel as her maid" (v 29). Indeed, it is the roughness with which these two verses have been forced into the narrative that spurs the reader to question their significance, and we soon realize that they warn of further troubles for Jacob's familial life. When Jacob finds himself married not only to the two sisters but to their two maidservants as well, his punishment grows twofold.

God, the master puppeteer, openly contributes to Jacob's predicament. Concerned for Leah, God wants to balance Jacob's relations with his wives—"The Lord saw that Leah was hated and he opened her womb; but Rachel was barren" (v 31)—only the elder sister's fertility and the younger's barrenness stir up domestic trouble. I have already mentioned the barren women among the patriarchal families: Sarah, who tried to hurry fate and secure a son by using her maidservant, and Rebekah, whose husband prayed for her and had his prayers answered. Let's see which recourse Rachel will choose when faced with her continuing barrenness.

God opens Leah's womb, leading to the birth of Jacob's first child. Jacob's sons become the patriarchs of the tribes of Israel so that, in the biblical epic, their births signify the transition from family to nation. The newborn's name, and Leah's explanation, which attributes meaning to its various sound components, are evidence that Leah recognizes God's role in her pregnancy and birth and is hopeful that the end of her suffering nears: "and she named him Re'uven for, she declared, The Lord *has seen* [*ra'ah*] *my affliction* [*be'onyi*], so now my husband will love me" (v 32). She doesn't dare hope that Jacob will love her for her own sake, and seems to think that her fertility is the only advantage she has over her sister. She will provide sons for her husband and, she believes, thereby secure his good opinion. Since her hopes for Jacob's love rest on her providing him with sons, the more the merrier: one birth follows quickly

upon the other, and Simeon, *Shim'on*, is soon born. Leah's etymology reveals how she no longer nurtures idle hopes for her
husband's affections: "This is because the Lord heard [*shama'*]
that I was hated and he has given me this one, too. And she
named him Shim'on" (v 33). Her emotional roller coaster continues with the next birth, when she looks back contentedly
on having borne Jacob three sons, a perfect and lucky number, and her optimism returns: "'This time my husband will
join [*yilaveh*] me, for I have borne him three sons.' And so she
named him Levi" (v 34). We cannot help but notice the un-
derlying revision in Leah's expectations: it is no longer "my
husband will love me" but merely that he "will join me," that
he will stand by her in gratitude since, through her, he has been
blessed with three sons. When her fourth son arrives, Leah
is certain of her victory over Rachel. Four quick births that
have produced four sons are enough, she believes, "and she
said, 'This time I will praise [*'odeh*] the Lord,' and so she named
him Judah. And she ceased bearing" (v 35). Leah praises God,
it is true, but she never expresses happiness for the sons themselves. Obsessed entirely with the competition with her sister,
Leah seems to regard her children as but the means to draw her
husband closer.

The birth of Judah represents the pinnacle of a literary-
numerical pattern widespread in the Bible and known as the
three-four pattern. In this pattern it is the fourth stage—the
stage beyond the perfect and complete third stage—that represents the essential and ultimate element toward which the
entire story is aimed. And indeed, Judah, Leah's fourth son, will
grow to be the patriarch of the foremost tribe, that from which
the House of David will spring, supplying the dynasty that will
rule in the Kingdom of Judah. But this is not the story's only or
final climax, as we will soon see.

Rachel's crushing defeat, her sister's four sons against her
inability to produce even a single child, triggers her jealousy

and fear of losing her husband: "When Rachel saw that she hadn't borne to Jacob, she was jealous of her sister . . ." (30:1). Notice that it doesn't say, "that she hadn't borne *children*," but "that she hadn't borne *to Jacob*," emphasizing how it was not a longing for motherhood that propelled her actions but something else. Rachel expects Jacob to help: "she was jealous of her sister and she said to Jacob, 'Give me sons or I shall die.'" Rachel's appetite is substantial. She needs more than one son because only that will give her equal status with Leah. Indeed, she says, without sons her life is not worth living. What does Rachel expect from Jacob? Rachel seems to expect him to do as Isaac did, when he prayed and his prayers were answered. But Jacob is indifferent to Rachel's pain; he already has four sons and doesn't particularly care who mothered them: "Jacob was incensed with Rachel, and said, 'Am I instead of God, who has denied you fruit of the womb?'" (v 2). Jacob's rhetorical question makes clear that he knows that only God can open a woman's womb, though he still does not turn to God in supplication. What's more, Jacob reminds her, God has prevented *her* from childbearing—not him; he has already been blessed with sons.

The same answer that Jacob gives Rachel will later be voiced in Egypt by Rachel's son Joseph to his guilt-ridden brothers, who fear his vengeance for their former brutality. When they plead to him to "forgive, we urge you, the crime and guilt of your brothers who treated you so harshly . . . ," Joseph answers, "Am I instead of God?" (50:17, 19). As always, the commonality between the two pictures prods us to notice their dissimilarity. When spoken by Jacob, the words reflect callousness toward his wife's distress. Joseph, in contrast, hears and appreciates the heartfelt words of his brothers. Because he is not God, he cannot injure them—even if he wanted to. What's more, the second story almost seems to provide the answer to the first. Whereas Rachel describes her wish to die

if her plea is not answered—"Give me sons or I shall die"—
Joseph knows that God's plan is meant to ensure life: "God
intended it for good, so as to bring this about, to keep alive an
abundant people" (50:20). The comparison between the two
episodes presents both Rachel and Jacob negatively—Rachel,
who made her demand, and particularly Jacob, who answered
impatiently, insensitively, and even with a lack of faith. The
brothers who appeal to Joseph for help, and especially Joseph,
who displays generosity and forgiveness toward them and con-
siders their evil behavior as part of a divine plan designed "to
keep alive an abundant people," are presented positively.

Back to our story. Rachel realizes that, unlike Isaac, Jacob
will not entreat God on her behalf, and she turns—as Sarah
did—to other means: "She said, 'Here is my maid Bilhah.
Consort with her, that she may bear on my knees and that
through her I too may have children'" (30:3). Now we begin
to comprehend, in retrospect, the verses about the father-in-
law's gift of the maidservants. Bilhah will give birth to Jacob's
children, whom Rachel will adopt and who, she thinks, will
relieve her suffering and shame. Rachel thus remembers Sarah
and her tactics but forgets (or tries to forget?) their unpleasant consequence: the birth of Ishmael and the jealousy engendered between Sarah and Hagar. She also seems to overlook
the possibility that Jacob might even come to love Bilhah. For
her, Bilhah represents but an available uterus, a means for her
to provide her husband with progeny. Jacob's consent to Rachel's proposal goes without saying: when it comes to women,
whether mother or wives, Jacob's passive acquiescence can be
assumed. Rachel, a woman of action, proceeds swiftly with her
plan: "So she gave him her maid Bilhah as concubine, and Jacob
cohabited with her" (v 4). Rachel succeeds (or so she believes):
Bilhah gives birth to a son, and Rachel is confident that God
approves of her actions: "And Rachel said, 'God has judged me
[*danani*]; indeed, He has heeded my plea and given me a son.'

Therefore she named him Dan" (v 6). God has indeed judged Rachel, though not necessarily in her favor, and her assumption that God has heeded her plea is premature: she will pay heavily for having tried to outmaneuver God.

Rachel demanded sons, not merely *a* son, so we are not really surprised when Bilhah quickly becomes pregnant and gives birth again. This time the name and its etymology reflect the bitter jealousy Rachel feels toward her fertile sister and the fact that this jealousy is what has driven her to want children: "And Rachel said, 'A fateful contest I waged [*naftulei . . . niftalti*] with my sister; yes, I have prevailed.' So she named him Naphtali" (v 8). She characterizes her struggle dramatically—"a fateful contest," literally, "a contest of God," that is, the ultimate contest, which has concluded successfully, in victory: "I have prevailed." This time she doesn't bother mentioning God's help: the victory is all hers.

Leah senses a threat from her sister's maneuverings and she decides to return fire with fire. She, too, received a maidservant from their father! "When Leah saw that she had stopped bearing, she took her maid Zilpah and gave her to Jacob as concubine" (v 9). Note: Leah doesn't bother to explain her motives to Jacob, nor does she wait for his consent; Jacob's submissiveness seems endless. Leah's stratagem meets with comparable success, and Zilpah gives birth to a son: "Leah said, 'Luck has come [*ba' gad*]!' And she named him Gad" (v 11). Gad is the name of the god of fate and luck (Isa 65:11), known to us from Aramaic documents, but Leah uses it to convey *her* good luck, which she does not attribute to God since it was with her own shrewdness, she contends, that she outwitted her sister. With the prompt birth of Zilpah's second child, Leah declares, "'I am happy [*be'oshri*]! for women have praised me ['*ishruni*].' So she named him Asher" (v 13). Once again we hear no expression of joy in motherhood, per se, but in recognition of her admirable position, achieved through the many sons she has produced.

This dizzying succession of births has prevented us from observing the rival sisters together on the same stage. The pace now slows a bit, and the two appear together, alone, for the first time, and we get to witness a conversation between them. Reuben, Leah's firstborn son, has found mandrakes in the field and has brought them to his mother (v 14). This is apparently an act of support for Leah in her struggle against her sister: folk belief credited the fruit with aphrodisiac powers and even the power to boost fertility. The fruit's name—*duda'im*— contributed to this belief, perhaps, since it closely resembles *dodim*, "love" (e.g., Prov 7:18). The two words appear together in Song of Songs: "Let us go early to the vineyards . . . There I will give my love [*dodai*] to you. The mandrakes [*duda'im*] yield their fragrance, at our doors are all choice fruits . . ." (7:13–14).

Rachel, aware of the mandrake's benefits, entreats Leah to "please give me some of your son's mandrakes" (v 14), but Leah still resents her younger sister: "Was it not enough for you to take away my husband, that you would also take my son's mandrakes?" (v 15). Does Leah refer to her having been Jacob's first wife? Has she forgotten that it was through subterfuge that Jacob married her instead of her sister? Or perhaps she protests Jacob's continued love for Rachel despite the many sons she has borne him? Whatever the cause, Rachel ignores Leah's accusation and offers a deal: "Therefore, let him lie with you tonight, in return for your son's mandrakes." Jacob, we now apprehend, has been spending his nights with Rachel, and his visit to Leah's bed will mark a departure from the normal routine. It is noteworthy that Rachel does not even consider consulting Jacob on whether he agrees to the arrangement; the compliant husband will not suddenly change his colors. And indeed, when Jacob returns from the field, he is approached by Leah, who has won the night with him: "You are to sleep with me, for I have hired you with my son's mandrakes" (v 16). Jacob wordlessly obeys: "And he lay with her that night." The expression

Leah uses, "for I have hired you" (*sakhor sekhartikha*), is revealing: she has purchased Jacob's services and he is nothing but a
sack of goods now being claimed by its owner. The two words
also serve as a covert explanation of the name given to the child
who will result from the evening's activities, Issachar, though
Leah will offer a very different etymology: "God heeded Leah,
and she conceived and bore him a fifth son. And Leah said,
'God has given me my reward [*sekhari*] for having given my
maid to my husband.' So she named him Issachar" (vv 17–18).
God indeed helps Leah and acknowledges her distress, but she
interprets His intervention incorrectly, as though giving Zilpah to Jacob was the right thing to do, and not an example of
anticipating God's will—an act that will bring trouble to the
household.

Rachel's attempt to mother a son with the aid of mandrakes
proves counterproductive: not only does she remain barren,
but her fertile sister beats her once again. The sisters' deal reminds us of a previous transaction between siblings, the exchange of the birthright for lentil porridge. In fact, the story of
the mandrakes is a reflection—a mirror image—of that other
transaction:

a. In the story of the birthright, what is purchased—lentil
   porridge—comes from the house, while the one who buys it
   has come in from the field: "Once when Jacob was cooking
   a stew, Esau came in from the field, exhausted . . ." (25:29).
   In the mandrake story, what is being sold comes from the
   field, and the purchaser is at home: "Once . . . Reuben
   came upon some mandrakes in the field and brought them
   to his mother Leah" (30:14).
b. In Genesis 25, the older brother wants what the
   younger has: "Stuff me with that red stuff" (v 30). In
   chapter 30, the younger sister wants something of the
   older sister's: "Please give me some of your son's mandrakes" (v 14).

   c. The younger brother wants something in exchange—the birthright: "Sell now your birthright to me" (v 31)—while the older sister's complaint implies her expectation of compensation, a night with her husband (30:15).

   d. Both buyers agree to the seller's terms: "And Esau said . . . of what use is my birthright to me?" (v 32); "Rachel replied, 'Therefore, let him lie with you tonight, in return for your son's mandrakes'" (30:15).

   e. The exchanges are completed. For the lentil stew that the younger brother gives his older brother, he receives the prize, the birthright: "he sold his birthright to Jacob. Jacob then gave Esau bread and lentil stew . . ." (vv 33–34). For the mandrakes she gives her younger sister, Leah wins the prize, their husband: " . . . And he lay with her that night" (30:16).

The episode of the mandrakes, therefore, carries a covert criticism of Jacob's purchase of the birthright, and is indeed one more measure-for-measure punishment. Just as Jacob takes advantage of his brother's hunger to purchase the birthright in exchange for a trivial fee—porridge—so does the unloved wife purchase relations with him in exchange for a negligible price: mandrakes. Moreover, Jacob, the slick negotiator in the first story, is transformed into negotiated goods in the second. As submissive as ever, Jacob provides sexual services for the purpose of procreating; he has become a stud, nothing more. In this way, one more account that was opened in Canaan—Jacob's despicable act, the purchase of the birthright from his brother—becomes settled in Haran.

   Leah's resumed childbearing does not cease after Issachar's birth: "And Leah conceived again and bore Jacob a sixth son" (v 19). The boy's name is given two explanations, two interpretations. In the first, which involves a loose phonetic similarity—"And Leah said, 'God has given me [*zevadani*] a choice gift [*zeved*]'" (v 20)—the mother offers thanks for the great gift that God has given her. In the second, in which the phonetic resemblance is closer, she resumes her previous tone, again regarding the birth as a means for securing her husband's commitment, even proudly tallying up the number of sons she has produced: "'This time my husband will exalt me [*yizbeleni*], for I have borne him six sons.' So she named him Zebulun." It is interesting that in her accounting, she has omitted the sons of her maidservant, Zilpah. Seeing as she herself has produced so many and her victory is indisputable, her disdain is directed at them, too.

As a sort of extra nod to Leah's victory, the story then recounts, briefly and unenthusiastically, that "Last, she bore him a daughter, and named her Dinah" (v 21). There is no explanation of the name: the daughter's birth is meant only to prepare us for a future episode in which she will be given a central role (a story we will discuss in chapter 7).

Leah's unrivaled supremacy over Rachel—six sons of her own and two of her maidservant's against the meager two sons of Rachel's maidservant—is proof of the pointlessness of Rachel's efforts to second-guess God's will and forestall her barren state, both by giving Jacob her maidservant and by using the mandrakes. Now that it is clear that neither stratagems nor manipulations will get her pregnant, God can attend to her suffering: "And God remembered Rachel and God heard her and opened her womb and she conceived and bore a son" (vv 22–23).

The birth of Joseph represents the second climax in the long saga of the births of Jacob's children (after Judah), and is the superior of the two: Joseph will father Ephraim, the tribe from which will be born Jeroboam, the founder of the Kingdom of Israel. But is Rachel joyful at the birth of her long-awaited son? The etymologies she gives his name provide an answer. In the first (in which the phonetic similarity is partial, at best), she rejoices at the respect that has finally been restored her, since she, too, is now a mother: "And she said, 'God has taken away ['*asaf*] my disgrace'" (v 23). Like her sister, Rachel expresses no feelings toward the newborn child. The second etymology (in which the phonetic similarity with the name *yosef* is complete) is even more outrageous: "May the Lord add [*yosef*] another son for me" (v 24). She has not even held the child to her breast and already she is back to her bad habits, competing fiercely with her sister. We are suddenly reminded of the intense jealousy that produced her demand to Jacob to "give me sons . . ." (30:1). Clearly she has remained determined not to be satisfied with only one son. She will pay a heavy price for this expectation.

The story of the birth of Jacob's sons has come to an end, though it is not finished. It might be claimed that the family has been richly blessed. Its rapid growth bodes well for the fulfillment of the divine plan to turn the patriarchal family into twelve tribes, into a great nation as numerous as "the stars in the heavens and as the sand . . . on the seashore" (Gen 22:17). But it is a mixed blessing: the multiple wives who bore Jacob's eleven (soon to be twelve) sons cast a long shadow onto the future, and the fear that the wives' mutual suspicions and jealousies will be passed to their sons is all too real. The story's two peaks, the births of Judah (the forefather of the kingdom that carries his name) and Joseph (the forefather of the Kingdom of Israel), pave the way for the bitter battle between them. Moreover, Jacob's submissiveness, his passive compliance throughout this period, bodes darkly for the future, too.

5

"Let me go and I will go to my place and to my land": Jacob's Odyssey from Slavery to Freedom

TWENTY YEARS of hard labor elapse between the day Jacob met Rachel by the well to when God finally removes her shame and opens her womb, leading to the birth of Joseph (as we learn from Gen 31:41). Now that Jacob and Rachel's union has finally borne fruit, Jacob can attend to unfinished business—the other reason for his flight to Haran—and return home from exile: "And it came to pass, when Rachel bore Joseph, that Jacob said to Laban: 'Let me go and I will go to my place and to my land'" (30:25). Jacob adds a further request: "Give me my wives and my children, for whom I have served you, that I may go, for you know the services I have rendered you" (v 26). Despite the exceedingly modest nature of his request, Jacob reminds his uncle-subjugator of the services he has performed for him in the hope that Laban will not harden his heart but will allow Jacob to leave Haran and return to Canaan. Perhaps

Jacob hoped, too, that his uncle and father-in-law would finally show a bit of generosity and actually pay him for his work.

Laban comprehends Jacob's meaning and, surprisingly, offers to pay him, even leaving it to Jacob to determine the amount due: "And Laban said to him, 'If, pray, I have found favor in your eyes, I have learned by divination that the Lord has blessed me because of you.' And he said, 'Name the wages due from me and I will pay you'" (vv 27–28). Notice how Laban's small speech is in two parts though there was no outside interruption. First he acknowledges what he has learned through inquiring of God, that it was because of Jacob that he prospered. The blessings Isaac gave his son back in Canaan, which have adhered to Jacob ever since, have proved beneficial to Laban as well. When Laban next opens his mouth, he acknowledges his responsibility to pay Jacob fairly. Of course, it is not out of the question that Laban's seemingly generous offer—that Jacob choose his own payment—represents nothing but a common opening position in Middle Eastern negotiating practices, like the opening offer of the Hittite Ephron to give Abraham the cave of Machpelah, in Hebron, for free. Those negotiations ended with Abraham making a sizable payment to Ephron of four hundred shekels of silver (23:10–15).

Jacob is in no hurry to present his claims. Instead, he repeats what he has already stated, "You know how I have served you and how your livestock has fared with me" (30:29), and then returns to the theme raised by Laban, that he was the reason for Laban's wealth: "For the little you had before I came has grown to much, since the Lord has blessed you wherever I turned. And now, when shall I make provision for my own household?" (v 30). Jacob's speech appears to have tested Laban's patience; he responds curtly, "What shall I pay you?" (v 31). But Jacob's answer is lengthy. First, he impresses his employer—this, too, a well-calculated, quintessential stage in bargaining—with the trivial nature of his request: "Pay me nothing if you will do this thing for me: Let me go back and herd your flocks and watch them" (v 31). As he goes on to specify the exact wages he expects, we begin to appreciate Jacob's cleverness: "Let me pass through your whole flock today, removing from there every speckled and spotted animal—every dark-colored sheep and every spotted and speckled goat. Such shall be my wages. In the future when you go over my wages, let my honesty toward you testify for me: if there are among my goats any that are not speckled or spotted or any sheep that are not dark-colored, they got there by theft" (vv 32–33). Though Jacob's contribution to Laban's wealth has been decisive, he asks only for the speckled goats and dark-colored sheep—not a large number since the vast majority of goats are black, and the sheep white. The clear distinction between black and speckled, and between white and black is such that, Jacob suggests, there will be no confusion when dividing up the flock and it will be nearly impossible for either side to cheat the other.

Laban is less than happy with Jacob's request. He agrees to the deal—"And Laban said, 'Let it be as you say'" (v 34)—but immediately sets about removing all the speckled goats and dark sheep from his herd and hands them over to his sons, whom he instructs to "put a three days'" distance between themselves and Jacob, who is left to herd the remaining flocks. Laban has not changed: he outsmarted Jacob when he switched his daughters on Jacob's wedding night, and now he tries again to outmaneuver him just as Jacob is about to leave. Laban knows that black goats will not produce multicolored goats and white sheep will not produce dark sheep, and he is smugly confident that Jacob will leave his house empty-handed.

But Laban has failed to accurately judge his rival. Though he successfully cheated Jacob in the past, Jacob's underhanded capabilities are well known. When he discovered Laban's previous deceit, Jacob could only complain (29:25); now he wastes no time with words. Using a procedure that seems based on folk belief and magic traditions, he peels off strips of bark from various sticks, which he then places in the water trough. The female goats will go into heat while facing the partially stripped sticks that are in the trough. Seeing their reflections in the water, their own images appearing spotted (because of the coinciding reflections of the sticks), the goats will conceive "streaked, spotted, and speckled young" (30:39), increasing Jacob's share. Jacob is careful to place the rods in the water only when the sturdier animals mate, not the weaker ones, so that he will receive the stronger offspring and leave the weaker to Laban (v 42). His scheme succeeds wildly, and his new wealth from the growing herd enables him to acquire "maidservants and menservants, camels and donkeys" (v 43).

We notice that Jacob did not pin his hopes on God but on his own cunning. His decision to rely on magic and shrewdness, and to avoid turning to heaven for help, may trigger our unease. We will soon see how it led some readers to expand the story.

Laban's sons openly express their jealousy: "Jacob has taken all that was our father's and from that which was our father's he has built up all this wealth" (31:1). Jacob is aware, too, of Laban's growing envy, strengthening our hero's determination to leave his father-in-law's house, a decision that receives divine validation: "Then the Lord said to Jacob, 'Return to the land of your fathers and to your birthplace and I will be with you'" (v 3). In these words we hear echoes of God's first command to the nation's first patriarch, Abraham: "Go forth from your land and from your birthplace and from your father's house to the land that I will show you" (12:1). Two of the nation's patriarchs have thus been commanded to go to Canaan: the first had to leave behind his father and his father's house, while the second must rejoin his father and his father's house. The words with which God ends his command to Jacob, "and I will be with you," reconfirm the blessing Jacob received at Bethel, "And behold, *I am with you;* I will protect you wherever you go and will return you to this land . . ." (28:15).

The encouragement God offers is not enough for Jacob, however; he wants to know that his wives will stand by him. He calls Rachel and Leah out to the field, far from the ears and eyes of their suspicious father. The interaction is an opportunity for us to hear Jacob venting his own anger against Laban: " . . . and you know that I have served your father with all my strength. And your father tricked me and changed my wages ten times, but God did not let him harm me" (31:6–7). Laban has deceived Jacob more than once regarding his salary: he has cheated him ten times!

As Jacob continues, what was previously presented as the magically induced increase of his flocks appears in an entirely new light: "If he said, 'The speckled shall be your wages,' then all the flocks bore speckled young; and if he said, 'The streaked shall be your wages,' then all the flocks bore streaked young" (v 8), all this being the manifestation of God's blessing: "God has taken your father's livestock and given it to me" (v 9). According to Jacob, it was not a combination of cunning and magic that increased his wages but an exasperated God who was acting against Laban's outrageous deceitfulness. Jacob's claim of divine intervention is based on a revelation he had in a dream: "Once, when the flocks were in heat, I raised my eyes and saw in a dream, and behold, the he-goats mounting the herd were streaked, speckled, and mottled . . . And in the dream an angel of God said to me, 'Jacob!' 'Here I am,' I answered, and he said, 'Raise your eyes and see all the he-goats that are mounting the flocks are streaked, spotted, and mottled, because I have seen all that Laban has been doing to you" (vv 10–12). Dreams relate to dreams, and the angel's next words refer us back to Jacob's actions after his other dream, in Bethel, before leaving Canaan: "I am the God Beth-el, where you anointed a pillar and where you made a vow to Me. Now, arise and leave this land and return to your native land" (v 13). According to this account, it was God who increased the population of streaked, spotted, and mottled flocks, not Jacob's manipulations.

Clearly, this second tradition, in Genesis 31, involving a flashback, was introduced in order to address readers' unease with Jacob's actions in chapter 30. In a Genesis scroll found at Qumran, as well as in the version of Genesis in the Samaritan Pentateuch, noticeable efforts have been made to tighten the correlation between the two traditions, the two different approaches, and make them tally. Thus, immediately following Laban's directions to his sons to distance all the colored herds and before recounting Jacob's response (his placing the sticks in the water trough, and so forth), the Qumran scroll and Samaritan Pentateuch inserted Jacob's dream from chapter 31, "And the angel of God came to Jacob in a dream, and he said, 'Jacob,' and he said, 'Here I am.' And he said, 'Lift up your eyes and see all the he-goats that are mounting the herds . . . ,'" thus presenting it as a divine command, which Jacob then obeys: "And Jacob took a fresh shoot of poplar, and of almond and plane, and he peeled strips in them . . ." (30:37).

The writer of Jubilees solved the problem of Jacob's magic manipulations simply. He removed Jacob from the scene: "And all the sheep produced lambs that were either spotted or speckled or grey, and they again produced lambs like themselves; and all that were spotted were Jacob's and those that were not were Laban's" (28:25–26).

Jacob's wives listen sympathetically to their husband as he complains about their father and offer their support: " . . . And they told him, 'Have we still a share in the inheritance of our father's house? Surely he regards us as outsiders, now that he has sold us and has used up our purchase price. Truly, all the wealth that God has taken away from our father belongs to us and to our children. Now then, do just as God has told you" (31:14–16). Their words substantiate Jacob's complaint and justify the steps he took to increase his share, as well as the planned departure—escape. And so, "Thereupon Jacob put his children and wives on camels; and he drove off all his livestock and all the wealth that he had amassed, the livestock in his possession that he had acquired in Paddan-Aram, to go to his father Isaac in the land of Canaan" (vv 17–18).

The long road to Jacob's father's house stretches before us, yet the storyteller first pauses to recount the circumstances surrounding the departure: "And Laban had gone to shear his sheep, and Rachel stole her father's household idols [*terafim*]. Jacob stole the heart of Laban the Aramean, not telling him that he was fleeing" (vv 19–20). The idols in question are figurines—they are Laban's "gods," as he himself will soon explain (v 30), which he uses for divination. Various verses in prophetic literature confirm this function of the terafim. Ezekiel mentions some of the king of Babylon's more popular divination techniques for decision-making: "For the king of Babylon has stood at the fork of the road, where two roads branch off, to perform divination: He has shaken arrows, consulted terafim, and inspected the liver" (Ezek 21:26). Zechariah claims that divination methods lie, "for the terafim spoke delusion, the augurs predicted falsely, and dreamers speak lies and console with illusions" (Zech 10:2). Laban, himself, has already mentioned his use of divination: " . . . I have learned by divination that the Lord has blessed me because of you" (30:27).

By stealing the terafim Rachel hopes to prevent her father from divining their route and discovering their whereabouts. Indeed, that was how her theft was interpreted in the midrash: "Why did she steal them? So that they will not say to Laban that Jacob flees with his wives and sons. [Does this mean that] the terafim speak? Yes, as it is written, 'for the terafim spoke delusion' [Zech 10:2], accordingly Rachel stole them" (*Tanḥuma, Vayetse* 12). While we may consider her theft to have been warranted, thievery is thievery, and she will be punished, as we will see.

The report of Rachel's theft is joined by a reference to Laban's heart being stolen by Jacob: "Jacob stole the heart of Laban the Aramean, not telling him that he was fleeing." The symmetry between verses 19 and 20, which each report an act of theft, was apparently an attempt to cleanse Jacob's reputation by implying that Rachel was the real thief, stealing an object, while Jacob stole nothing actual from Laban. If he nonetheless became stuck with the label "thief," it was only because he "stole" Laban's heart when he "stole away" without telling him.

When Laban learns of Jacob's flight, he sets out in pursuit and, after seven days, catches up to the group on Mount Gilead. Rachel's theft has apparently done little to help them escape her father's wrath. It is the intervention of God, who appears to Laban in a dream and warns him to "beware of speaking with Jacob, good or bad" (v 24), that somewhat tempers Laban's anger.

Laban begins with accusations: "What did you mean by stealing my heart and carrying off my daughters like captives of the sword? Why did you flee in secrecy and steal me? I would have sent you off with festive music, with timbrel and lyre. You did not even let me kiss my sons and daughters good-by! It was a foolish thing for you to do" (vv 26–28). We are not fooled by Laban's pretense of being a loving father since we already heard his daughters telling Jacob that " . . . surely he regards us as outsiders . . ." (vv 15–16). We also notice how the father-in-law's allegations change and intensify: while he first blames Jacob only with stealing his heart, in the very next breath he refashions it into "steal me."

Laban's accusations are grave, but he is careful and admits that Jacob's God has tempered his response: "My hand has the power to do you harm, but the God of your fathers spoke to me last night, saying, 'Watch yourself, lest you speak to Jacob either good or evil'" (v 29). Mentioning Jacob's God reminds Laban of his own, the terafim that were stolen from him, and he proceeds to his second accusation: "You had to leave because you so strongly longed for your father's house, but why did you steal my gods?" (v 30).

Jacob responds with a clean conscience, questioning Laban's character and capacity for deceit: "For I was afraid, because I thought you would steal your daughters from me" (v 31). Quite so!—Jacob is saying—If indeed, as you yourself say, you are a loving father, the danger is all the more real that you would take them from me (particularly in light of the deceit that we already know you capable of). Regarding the stolen gods, Jacob answers with conviction: "With whomever you find your gods, that person shall not live; in front of our kinsmen, recognize what of yours is with me and take it" (v 32). Jacob's confidence, the omniscient storyteller next explains, stems from the fact that "Jacob did not know that Rachel had stolen them." The clarification is meant to clear him entirely of guilt in the theft, while his words " . . . shall not live" will prove prophetic: Rachel will die before their journey reaches its end.

Laban understands Jacob's declaration "with whomever you find your gods . . ." as permission to conduct a search, leaving readers tense with anticipation: will Laban find the thief? Since Jacob is Laban's prime suspect, he begins with Jacob's tent. Dramatic tension is heightened as the storyteller leaves Rachel's tent for last: "And Laban came to Jacob's tent and to Leah's tent and to the tent of the two maidservants and didn't find it. And he left Leah's tent and came to Rachel's tent" (v 33). Only then, by way of a flashback, does the storyteller reveal what Rachel has done to prevent discovery: "And Rachel had taken the terafim and put them in the camel cushion and sat on them" (v 34). Her plan succeeds. Laban searches but finds nothing, while his daughter, sitting serenely on her pillows, lies outright: "Let not my lord be angry that I cannot rise before you, for the way of women is upon me" (v 35).

As an aside, not every reader seems to have looked askance

at Rachel's thievery. We see this indirectly by way of a different story apparently influenced by ours: David's escape from King Saul with the help of his wife, Saul's daughter, Michal (don't forget that Saul and Michal were from the tribe of Benjamin— Rachel's son).

> Michal let David down from the window and he escaped and fled. Michal then took the *terafim*, laid it on the bed, and covered it with a cloth; and at its head she put a net of goat's hair. Saul sent messengers to seize David, but she said, "He is sick." Saul, however, sent back the messengers to see David for themselves. "Bring him up to me in the bed," he ordered, "that he may be put to death." When the messengers came, they found the household idol in the bed, with the net of goat's hair at its head. Saul said to Michal, "Why did you play that trick on me and let my enemy get away safely?" (1 Sam 19:11–17)

A number of likenesses draw our attention. Both stories tell of a daughter who betrays her father's trust; terafim, household gods, are used in both accounts to help in the escape. Rachel's alleged condition, her false claim of her menstrual period, prevented the idols' discovery, while Michal's false claim of David's illness sabotaged, if only temporarily, the discovery of David's flight.

There are notable differences between the episodes—another example of the inverse relationships that were a favorite of the biblical writers. In Genesis, the terafim disappear, while in 1 Samuel it appears and David disappears. Rachel's theft goes undiscovered, whereas Saul discovers Michal's deceit and blames her for it. Jacob, as we've already mentioned, speaks truthfully, if unknowingly, when he says, "With whomever you find your gods, that person shall not live," while Michal lies to her father when she tells him that "[David] said to me, 'Help me get away or I will kill you.'" Finally, Rachel dies with the birth of her second son, Benjamin (Gen 35:17–20), whereas

Michal lives a long—though childless—life (2 Sam 6:23). This connection between the stories seems to have been shaped by the writer of the later one, in 1 Samuel, who appears to have approved of Rachel and the steps she took to help her husband. He used Rachel as a template with which to portray Michal as a similar but stronger heroine: while Rachel—who admittedly takes a certain personal risk—flees along with her husband, Michal is left behind knowing that her role in the escape will certainly be discovered and that she will be left to confront her father alone.

Let us return now to Jacob, who is about to reunite with his brother. Laban's failure to find the terafim fills Jacob with confidence and he rushes to point the finger back at his father-in-law. His bitter words shed light on the long years of his servitude: "And Jacob became angry and he voiced his grievance to Laban, and Jacob spoke up and said to Laban, 'What is my crime? What is my guilt that you should chase me? You rummaged through all my things; what did you find of all your household things? Set it here before my kin and your kin and they shall decide between us two'" (Gen 31:36–37). Laban's failed search has confirmed Jacob's claim of integrity, which, in his eyes, was the natural continuation of his past—"These twenty years I have been with you, your ewes and she-goats never miscarried, nor did I eat the rams from your flock. That which was torn by beasts I did not bring to you; I myself made good the loss; you exacted it of me, whether stolen by day or stolen by night" (vv 38–39). Jacob's watchful care of Laban's flocks was what had prevented them from miscarrying. Nor did he help himself to any meat on Laban's account, and when any of the flocks were stolen, Jacob paid for the losses from his own pocket. Even when an animal was killed by a wild beast, Jacob hadn't abandoned his responsibility to replace the goat or sheep, an allowance granted him by law ("If it was torn by beasts, he shall bring it as evidence; he need not replace what has been torn by beasts" [Exod 22:12; see also Amos 3:12]). Dutifully safeguarding Laban's flocks, Jacob was exposed to harsh conditions, day and night: "Often, scorching heat ate me and ice, at night, and sleep wandered from my eyes" (v 40). Now we finally learn the number of years that Jacob toiled so loyally in Laban's service: "It has been twenty years I have worked in your house, fourteen years for your two daughters, and six years for your flocks" (v 41). When Jacob asked for his wages, therefore, he was not asking for charitable kindness on Laban's part but payment for six years of work, and it was these wages that the ingrate Laban was trying to cheat him out of, "and you switched my wages ten times," an accusation Jacob previously made before his wives. God, in His providence, had prevented Laban from abusing Jacob: "Were it not that the God of my father, the God of Abraham and the Terror of Isaac [a nickname of God, the fear of whom fell on Laban] was with me, you would now have sent me off empty-handed" (v 42), in violation of the custom, according to which slaves were paid when freed (Deut 15:13).

Jacob has interpreted God's intervention, revealed in Laban's dream, as expressing the victory of God's providence, which prevents injustice against the weak by the more powerful: "God took notice of my plight and the toil of my hands, and He gave judgment last night" (v 42). When we first learned of God's dream-delivered warning (in v 29), we might have thought that God had arbitrarily sided with Jacob, but Jacob explains that it was the Law of Retribution at work. He has learned his lesson, first through the switching of the daughters and then with twenty years of servitude, that both Justice and Judge exist, and that one's every action will be measured and judged accordingly. Charged with a sin that he did not commit, Jacob voices his faith in God's justice, which will not allow Laban to harm him.

Hearing Jacob's emotional words, Laban changes his tune.

He understands that time cannot be reversed and that Jacob will no longer be under his power. Nonetheless, he, too, wishes to end the confrontation on the moral high ground, as the generous one who willingly waives his rights: "and Laban answered Jacob, saying, 'The daughters are my daughters and the sons are my sons and the flocks are my flocks, and all that you see is mine. What will I do to my daughters today or to the children that they have borne?'" (v 43). But we are unconvinced: his character has been modeled after Pharaoh, the king of Egypt, the one who enslaved the Israelites. It is no coincidence that a midrash in the Passover haggadah compares the two, to the benefit of Pharaoh: "What did Laban the Aramean try to do to our father Jacob? Pharaoh condemned only the male (children) but Laban sought to uproot them all."

Laban was indeed modeled after the cruel figure of Pharaoh, and the Exodus from Egypt, the decisive event in Israel's formation as a nation, left its mark on our chapter about Jacob's departure from Laban's house. We find its imprint everywhere. We notice, for example, how Jacob is initially received into Laban's house graciously, as are Jacob and his sons when they first arrive in Egypt. Afterward, Jacob—like the Israelites—becomes enslaved by his host. Jacob manages to establish an extensive family in Haran, a family that multiplies and becomes a people in Egypt. Genesis 30:43 employs the root *p-r-ts* to describe the tremendous growth of Jacob's property, "So the man *expanded greatly* and came to have many flocks, maidservants and menservants, camels and donkeys"; in Exodus 1:12 the same root is used to refer to the growth of Israel, the nation, in Egypt: "But the more they were oppressed the more they increased *and expanded.*" In both stories the host/oppressor tries to prevent this growth: Laban tries to swindle Jacob out of his wages, while Pharaoh tries to kill the male Israelites.

God sees the suffering of Jacob and the Israelites and commands both of them to return to their land, the Land of Canaan. Compare Genesis 31:12–13—"And he said, '. . . for *I have seen* all that Laban has been doing to you . . . Now, arise and leave this land and return to your native land'"—with Exodus 3:7–8: "And God said, '*I indeed have seen* the plight of my people in Egypt and have heeded their outcry because of their taskmasters, for I know their suffering. I have come down to rescue them from the Egyptians and to bring them out of that land to a good and spacious land, a land flowing with milk and honey, to the place of the Canaanite . . .'" The suffering of the oppressed leads to an appeal for release: "And Jacob said to Laban, '*Let me go* and I will go to my place and to my land'" (Gen 30:25). God directs Moses to pronounce almost identical words to Pharaoh: "*Let my people go* that they may worship Me . . ." (Exod 7:16). What's more, in both cases slavery ends with the enslaved receiving payment before leaving. In both stories we find the root *n-ts-l* being used: Jacob tells his wives, "God has taken away [*vayatsel*] your father's livestock and given it to me" (Gen 31:9), while God instructs Moses, "Each woman shall borrow from her neighbor and the lodger in her house objects of silver and gold, and clothing, and you shall put these on your sons and daughters, thus you shall take away from [*venitsaltem*] the Egyptians" (Exod 3:22; see also 12:26).

Both hosts/oppressors are inconstant: Laban changes Jacob's wages ten times and in Exodus it takes ten plagues to convince Pharaoh that he should let the Israelites leave Egypt. In the end, the enslaved have no choice but to flee their oppressors: "Jacob stole the heart of Laban the Aramean, not telling him that he was *fleeing*. And he *fled*, he and all that he had, and he rose and crossed the river . . ." (Gen 31:20–21). The same term for fleeing, *b-r-ḥ*, appears in Exodus 14:5.

Finally, I note two more parallels. The discovery of the flight is reported identically in both stories—"And . . . was told that . . . had fled" (Gen 31:22; Exod 14:5)—as is the subsequent pursuit: "So [Laban] *took* his kinsmen with him and *chased after* him a distance of seven days" (Gen 31:22); "[Pharaoh] *took* six hundred of his picked chariots, and the rest of the chariots of Egypt with officers in all of them. The Lord stiffened the heart of Pharaoh king of Egypt, and he *chased after* the Israelites" (Exod 14:7–8). This accumulation of correspondences insistently depicts Laban as a Pharaoh-like, cruel oppressor from whom Jacob had no choice but to escape.

Let's return to Jacob and Laban, as they confront one another on the heights of Mount Gilead. Now that both have presented themselves as righteous, the time has come to make a pact, an agreement between equals. These two men, who have repeatedly tried one another with acts of trickery, need a covenant, a legal procedure that will guarantee that all maneuverings and deceit between them will cease. As witness to the pact, they gather a pile of stones and erect a pillar. Laban gives the pile of stones an Aramaic name, *Yegar-sahadutha*—these are the only Aramaic words in the entire Torah—while Jacob uses the Hebrew equivalent, *Gal-ed* (v 47), both terms meaning "mound of witness." The Hebrew functions as a covert etymology of the place: *har hagilad*, "Mount Gilead" (v 25). Jacob then erects the pillar (*matsevah;* v 45) and it, too, has an etymological function, since the place is given the name *Mitspeh* Gilead (see Judg 11:29), as said by Laban: "And [it was called] *Mitspah*, because he said, 'May the Lord watch [*yitsef*] between you and me'" (v 49).

The pillar that Jacob erects constitutes one more connection between the closing scene of Jacob's journey and its beginning, twenty years earlier. We already saw how, just before leaving Haran, God alerted and encouraged Jacob in a dream that alluded to the dream-revelation Jacob had had previously, at Bethel, in which he had been told to leave Laban's house and return to his land: "I am the God Bethel, where you anointed a pillar and where you made a vow to Me. Now, arise and leave this land and return to your native land" (v 13). Now, as Jacob stands at the border between Laban's land and the land promised him and his descendants, he again erects a pillar.

Laban, who initiates the pact, presents its two parts. First, he again depicts himself as a caring father whose only concern is his daughters' well-being, as though Jacob had threatened them: "If you ill-treat my daughters or take other wives besides my daughters—though no one else be about, remember, God Himself will be witness between you and me" (v 50).

Second, he establishes a border between the two nations:

> Here is this mound and here the pillar which I have set up between you and me: this mound [*gal*] shall be witness and this pillar [*matsevah*] shall be witness that I am not to cross to you past this mound, and that you are not to cross to me past this mound and this pillar, with hostile intent. May the god of Abraham and the god of Nahor judge between us. (vv 51–53)

Rocks and pillar function, therefore, as borders between the two nations, and the gods of both, which protect their respective territories, are witnesses to the pact's formation and the nations' compliance with it. More than anything else, this seems to reflect Israel's aspiration that the border between Israel and Aram would pass through Gilead, perhaps at Mitspeh Gilead. And since it is Laban who suggests this significance of the mound and pillar, his descendants, the Arameans, would be hard put to disavow their forefather's declaration and violate his pledge by crossing the border and invading Israel's territory.

Relations on the Israel-Aram border were particularly strained during the period of the Israelite monarchy in the ninth century b.c.e., when King Ahab sought to recapture Ramoth-gilead from the Arameans, certain that it was in Israelite territory (1 Kings 22:3). His son Joram, we are later told, "had been defending Ramoth-gilead against King Hazael of Aram" (2 Kings 9:14). The story of the pact between Laban and Jacob, therefore, would seem to have been written during a period of skittish relations between the kingdoms, by a writer who claimed Israelite sovereignty over the disputed area—as agreed to in the treaty between the two forefathers.

Following the customary, concluding ceremony, which included a sacrifice and shared meal (compare the ceremony at the conclusion of the pact between Isaac and Abimelech, king of Gerar, in Gen 26:30), Laban and Jacob part ways. At this moment readers finally believe Laban's sincerity; he embraces his children wholeheartedly, knowing that he will never see them again: "And Laban rose early in the morning and he kissed his sons and his daughters and he blessed them, and Laban returned to his place" (32:1).

Jacob, too, heads on his way (v 2), preparing himself for closure in yet another sphere: facing Esau for the first time since he purchased his brother's birthright and stole his blessing.

6

"*For you have striven with God and with men
and have prevailed*": *Jacob's Homebound Encounters*

THE NEXT segment of Jacob's biography is perhaps the most complicated, though the problem is not in the events themselves, which are rather straightforward: Jacob parts from Laban and, after a brief encounter with some angels (told in half a verse) at a place he then calls Mahanaim, he prepares for the much-anticipated meeting with his brother. He sends messengers ahead with explicit instructions and a sizable gift, and he camps for the night alongside the Jabbok River. That night Jacob meets another divine being who wrestles with him and changes his name to Israel, after which Jacob names the place Penuel. Finally, Esau and his entourage approach and the reunion between the brothers is, to Jacob's great relief, a warm one. Jacob's gifts are accepted and there is reconciliation.

Our confusion—perplexity, even—arises when we look critically at the biblical text and realize that the writers were laboring to hide something. Indeed, much of our time in this chapter will be spent clearing away a web of strange traditions that were formed as damage control, meant to steer readers clear of a particularly ancient and dangerous tradition about a human hero who wrestled with—and claimed victory over—a divine being. Jacob's return will also leave its stamp on the map of Israel, which, marked with the names he leaves behind, will forever remind us of his experiences. Even Jacob's own name will be changed at the beginning of this new phase of his life. Who knows: perhaps we will discover that our hero's character will have been transformed as well, after his long and difficult years of slavery and exile. But let us begin at the beginning.

When Jacob first left his father's house and native land, his departure was prompted by two causes: he fled *from* his brother's wrath, but he also traveled *toward* Haran, with the aim of finding a wife. Now that he has left Haran, we see how this parting, too, has a dual purpose: he flees Laban, running from his father-in-law's cruel treatment, but he also sets out toward something, a return to his own father and land.

As long as Jacob's mind was occupied with leave-taking, there was little time to contemplate what awaited him. But now, as the exile chapter—the Laban chapter—of his life has ended and Jacob takes his first steps back into vistas long forgotten, his mind must be flooded with apprehension and concern: Has his brother's rage subsided? Are his elderly parents still alive?

Jacob's first encounter occurs once he and Laban part ways and he is on the path that will take him across the Jordan— "And Jacob went on his way" (32:2)—to which the writer-editor has attached a brief if peculiar note: "And angels of God came upon him. When he saw them, Jacob said, 'This is God's camp [*maḥaneh 'elohim*].' So he named that place Mahanaim" (vv 2–3). Mahanaim (*maḥanaim*), a city in Gilead on the eastern side of the Jordan, will serve important functions in Israel's future: it is from here that Ish-boshet, the son of King Saul, will rule over Israel (2 Sam 2:8); David will find refuge here on his flight from his rebellious son Absalom (2 Sam 17:24 ff.); and one of Solomon's prefects will use Mahanaim as his base (1 Kings 4:14). Jacob's encounter with angels here, just before entering the Land of Israel, reminds us of his dramatic dream in Bethel on the night of his escape in the opposite direction, when he watched God's angels ascending and descending. The resemblance between the two encounters is further signaled by shared terminology. There we read: "And he came upon [*vayifga*'] the place and stopped there" (28:11), and here: "And angels of God came upon [*vayifge'u*] him" (32:2). We also recall another appearance of an angel to Jacob, again in a dream, when he was in Haran and the angel instructed him to return to his native land (31:12–13). Indeed, Jacob seems to have been the beneficiary of a somewhat constant angel escort. This was why the midrash (see the *Genesis Rabbah* passage I cited in chapter 3) understood the ascending and descending angels as a "changing of the guard": the changeover between those angels that accompanied him in his own land and those responsible for guarding him outside Israel. According to the Rabbis, now that Jacob has returned to his native land, the Israel team of angels seems again to be taking their places.

In any case, it seems that this short and rather abrupt tradition about a sudden meeting at Mahanaim hides something larger: Is it only by chance that the writer used the verb *vayifge'u*? The verb has a double meaning. The *peshat* here is "to encounter," but the more common meaning suggests danger—"to harm, cause injury" (Judg 18:25). By using the verb here—where the angels plainly caused Jacob no harm—the writer manages to simultaneously suggest and deny any notion that it attacked Jacob. Our storyteller hints at a tradition, well known to his audience, about a fierce struggle between Jacob and God's representatives, a tradition in which Jacob acquired dimensions of a mythological hero with the power to triumph over divine beings. This writer wanted to deny that such a violent encounter took place, to neutralize the tradition about a struggle with divine beings at Mahanaim, by deliberately using the ambiguous verb: yes, he implies, a "confrontation" occurred, but it was a peaceful *encounter*, a meeting with angels signifying that their master—God—was near—"This is God's camp"—like at Bethel, when the vision of angels preceded Jacob's audience with God.

The short episode that provides this overt etymology of Mahanaim has become appended to a longer story recounting the meeting between Jacob and Esau and interpreting the name Mahanaim once more, this time covertly. The word *mal'akhim*, meaning both "angels" and "messengers," connects the two stories, as Jacob dispatches *mal'akhim* to his brother in Edom and directs them: "Thus you shall say to my lord, to Esau: 'Thus said your servant Jacob: With Laban I have dwelled and stayed until now'" (32:5). Jacob wants to placate his brother. Having taken the birthright and stolen the blessing that made him his brother's master, he now makes a gesture of deep obeisance: he is no longer master but servant. He also fears his brother's wrath. His messengers are told to tell of Jacob's wealth: "I have acquired cattle, asses, sheep, and male and female slaves; and I send this message to my lord in the hope of gaining your favor" (v 6), discreetly signaling Jacob's readiness to purchase Esau's forgiveness by dividing his property with him.

But the messengers return with no message and their report is troubling: "We came to your brother Esau; he himself is coming to meet you, and there are four hundred men with him" (v 7). The number inspires fear since it is the size of a militia heading to battle (see, e.g., 1 Sam 22:2; 25:13; 30:10): "Jacob was greatly frightened, and he was anxious, and he divided the people that were with him, and the flocks and herds and camels, into two camps [*shnei maḥanot*]. And he thought, If

Esau comes to the one camp [*maḥaneh*] and attacks it, the other camp [*maḥaneh*] may yet escape" (vv 8–9). Jacob's response represents a covert etymology of Mahanaim, interpreting it as though it carried the dual suffix (*-aim*) and signified *two camps*. Unlike the place's overt etymology, "God's camp," this one bears no trace of any sort of heavenly connection and certainly not to any physical struggle taking place there. It distances us even further from the violent-encounter tradition by defining Mahanaim in purely secular terms, while the reader who hears of Jacob's trepidation as he awaits his brother will find it hard to imagine this same person being brave enough to challenge divine beings.

Jacob may fear his impending meeting with Esau but he knows how to proceed. Quickly and decisively, he offers a prayer to God, "Oh God of my father Abraham and God of my father Isaac, O Lord, who said to me, 'Return to your native land and I will deal bountifully with you'" (v 10). This opening mentions the command/promise God made to Jacob when Jacob had been in Haran—"Return to the land of your fathers and to your birthplace and I will be with you'" (31:3)—and contains an echo, too, of God's reference to Himself in Jacob's stairway dream, "I am the Lord, the God of your father Abraham and the God of Isaac" (28:13), and the promise He made then, to "return you to this land. I will not leave you . . ." (v 15). God's promise requires that He protect Jacob from Esau. Jacob's aim in the next part of his prayer is to stir God's favor by showing his gratitude: "I am unworthy of all the kindness that You have steadfastly shown your servant. For with my staff I crossed the Jordan and now I have become two camps [*shnei maḥanot*]" (v 11). In repeating the covert etymology for Mahanaim, Jacob confers one more dimension of meaning: the "two camps" are a manifestation of the abundant possessions he brings with him, in contrast to when he left Canaan with only the staff in his hand.

Now that Jacob has recalled previous instances of divine help, he makes explicit his current request: "Save me, please, from the hand of my brother, from the hand of Esau, for I fear him lest he come and strike me, mother together with sons" (v 12). The phrase "mother together with sons" connotes unparalleled brutality. Its particular wording is found in only one other biblical verse, in the law that forbids taking both mother and offspring from a bird's nest: "If . . . you chance upon a bird's nest . . . do not take the mother together with her young [*ha'em 'al habanim*]" (Deut 22:6–7).

Jacob seals the prayer by returning and adding to his initial reminder: "Yet You Yourself said, 'I will surely deal bountifully with you and make your offspring as the sands of the sea, which cannot be counted for their numerousness" (v 13). Compare this to God's promise in Jacob's stairway dream, "and your seed shall be as the dust of the earth . . ." (28:14), and God's promise to Abraham that "I will surely make your seed as numerous as the stars in the heavens and as the sand that is on the seashore . . ." (22:17). Jacob's abundant offspring and property are proof that God's promise has already begun to be fulfilled: God can hardly stop now before completing the blessing's realization.

The prayer seems to have revived Jacob's strength. After sleeping the night, he turns to prepare a sizable gift (*minḥah*) for his brother, " . . . and he took from what he had at hand a gift for Esau, his brother" (v 14). The term used in both this and the coming verses (*minḥah*; vv 19, 21, 22) serves as one more covert interpretation of Mahanaim, this time by a transposition of the letters. The storyteller specifies the exact numbers of animals Jacob will give his brother, in order to amaze us with the patriarch's wealth and generosity: "Two hundred she-goats and twenty he-goats; two hundred ewes and twenty rams; thirty milch camels with their young; forty cows and ten bulls; twenty she-asses and ten he-asses" (vv 15–16). To impress Esau and awaken his interest, Jacob readies the shepherds of his flocks to intercept his brother. First, he instructs them to make their way before him, leaving space between droves (v 17). The spacing will play a role in both possible scenarios: similar to the division of his property and people into two camps, it precludes a total loss should Esau be planning an attack, in which case only one herd would be harmed and the rest would manage to flee. If Esau's intentions are peaceful, however, the spacing will prove equally effective: Esau will think that he has seen all of Jacob's property, only to be astounded when wave after wave of animals and shepherds continue to approach.

Jacob even equips his men with the precise words for any possible questioning:

> He instructed the one in front as follows, "When my brother Esau meets you and asks you, 'Whose man are you? Where are you going? And whose are these [herds] before you?' you shall answer, 'Your servant Jacob's; they are a gift sent to my lord Esau; and behold, he is right behind us.'" He gave similar instructions to the second one, and the third and all the others who followed the herds, namely, "In this way you shall speak to Esau when you find him. And you shall say, 'And your servant Jacob himself is right behind us.'" For he thought, "If I make amends with a gift that goes before me and only afterwards look on his face, perhaps he will show me favor." (vv 18–21)

Jacob finally acknowledges guilt, "If I make amends," and expresses hope that Esau will, with great generosity, forgive his past transgressions: "perhaps he will show me favor." The scene of Jacob dispatching the gift to Esau (vv 14–21) ends how it began: "And the gift passed on before him, and he spent that night in the camp" (v 22).

But this is really the beginning of another scene, another meeting between Jacob and a divine being, this time just as we are anticipating the reunion with Esau. What was completely obscured in the meeting with the holy beings at Mahanaim becomes more apparent here, where the existence of a struggle is admitted:

> And that night he got up and took his two wives and his two maidservants and his eleven sons and he crossed the Jabbok [*yaboq*] ford. And he took them and they crossed the river and he brought across all that he had. And Jacob was left alone and a man wrestled [*vaye'aveq*] with him until the break of dawn. (vv 23–25)

Jacob's adversary is a man, *'ish*, a term used regularly to refer also to angels (see the alternate uses of the term in the Sodom and Gomorrah story: "men," in Gen 18:2, 16, 22; 19:5, 8, 10, 12, 16; "angels" in 19:1, 15). The match with the "man" takes place at a ford of the Jabbok, one of the tributaries of the Jordan that joins it about forty kilometers north of the Dead Sea. The story interprets the river's name, *yaboq*, as derived from the root *'-b-q*, "to wrestle, struggle," which makes its single appearance in the Bible in this episode (v 25; see also v 26).

The episode preserves the more ancient elements of a mythical tradition about a perilous confrontation involving a hero who must confront a divine (or demonic) being(s) at the crossing point between two territories. Indeed, Jacob's encounter with his divine adversary just as he is about to enter the Land of Israel will be repeated by Moses, who will find himself facing a similar threat on his way from Midian to Egypt in one of the Bible's most bizarre episodes: "And it happened on the way at the night camp that the Lord met him and sought to kill him. And Zipporah took a flint and cut off her son's foreskin and touched his legs with it and she said, 'A bridegroom of blood you are to me!' And He let him alone . . ." (Exod 4:24–26). In our story, however, the crux has been somewhat blunted by Jacob's adversary being initially depicted as a "man" and not God (though he will be called that in verse 29). In the struggle, Jacob proves his superior strength:

And he [the divine creature] saw that he had not prevailed and he touched his [Jacob's] hip at its socket, so that the socket of his hip was strained as he wrestled with him. Being that even that injury did not cause the determined Jacob to let his rival go, that one pleaded, "Let me go, for dawn is breaking." And he said, "I will not let you go unless you bless me." And he said to him, "What is your name?" And he said, "Jacob." And he said, "No longer Jacob shall your name be said, but Israel for you have striven with God and with men and have prevailed." And Jacob asked, saying, "Tell me, pray, your name?" And he said, "Why do you ask my name?" And he blessed him there. (vv 26–30)

When his grip does not cause the resolute Jacob to relent, the angel implores, "Let me go, for dawn is breaking" (v 27), a remnant of a folk belief in the nocturnal nature of demonic spirits who are unable to show themselves in daytime. Jacob's stubborn determination is apparent also when he asks the being, whom he perceives as divine, for a blessing. Jacob's appetite for blessings has not diminished, nor have his negotiating skills. Something *has* shifted, however, in that he no longer attempts to secure blessings through deceit.

Ancients and moderns alike have puzzled over this powerful episode, this nocturnal confrontation between the somewhat reformed Jacob and the mysterious and anonymous being. The cluster of interactions that Jacob experiences in these chapters, all in close geographic proximity to one another, begins to reveal a pattern. Particularly here, the history of the story seems important, a history that we are able to recover through close analysis of the text. Something feels slightly uneven in the verses that relate Jacob's name change from Jacob to Israel, where the progression from the end of verse 27, " . . . unless you bless me," to verse 30b, "and he blessed him there," appears to be the natural one. This leads us to suspect that the verses in between, which relate the name change, were added at a secondary stage (though, as we'll soon see, threatening confrontations and name changes tend to go together). As the text now stands, the man-angel asks the name of his opponent before blessing him, and when he is told "Jacob," he replies: "No longer Jacob shall your name be said, but Israel [*yisra'el*] for *you have striven* with *God* [*sarita* . . . *'elohim*] and with men and have prevailed" (v 29).

The name change, denoting a change of destiny, continues the patriarchal tradition that began with the change from Abram to Abraham (Gen 17:5) and Sarai to Sarah (vv 15–16). In our story, the root *'-k-b* (*ya'aqov*) is exchanged for *s-r-h* (*sarita*). In order to account for the ultimate syllable in the name *yisra'el*, the text admits that Jacob wrestled *with God* (*'im 'elohim*): Jacob is the one who "strove with God"! In order to immediately obscure this shocking assertion, however, the words "and with men" were added. A reader who cannot accept the notion that Jacob fought with God can interpret the prefixed *vav* not as a connective conjunction ("and") but as an appositive *waw*, as though it were written, "you strove with gods, that is, men" (which could also mean "divine creatures" and refer to angels).

Despite Jacob's expectation of some sort of reciprocal frankness, the being is unwilling to reveal his name—"Jacob asked, saying, 'Tell me, pray, your name.' And he said, 'Why do you ask my name?'" (v 30a)—reminding us of the experience of Manoah, Samson's father: "And Manoah said to the angel of God, 'What is your name, so that when your words prove true, we can honor you?' And the angel of the Lord said to him, 'Why do you ask my name, for it is wondrous'" (Judg 13:17–18). Two considerations appear to lie behind the being's reticence: first, the being knows his name might have endowed Jacob with some sort of power over him; second, the Bible (except for the late Book of Daniel) resists naming angels or giving them any sort of individuality in order to prevent their becoming objects of worship.

Even if we accept the etymology of Israel as integral to the episode, the same cannot possibly be said for the explanation given the name Peniel, a town adjacent to the Jabbok, in the episode's next words: "So Jacob called the place Peniel, 'For I have seen God face to face [*panim 'el panim*] and my life has been preserved'" (v 31). This explanation was added because of Penuel's mention in the next verse: "The sun rose upon him as he passed Penuel, limping on his hip," but it is at odds with the story itself. While the tradition tells of a fierce struggle, the etymology refers to an encounter involving only visual contact. It resembles the overt etymology of Mahanaim in Genesis 32:2b–3, which also speaks of a visual encounter—and no more—with angels. Both etymological traditions are part of the arsenal of stories used to combat the ancient tradition of a physical struggle.

Because the encounter—according to the writer of this etymology of Penuel—involved only seeing, it could involve God as Jacob's opponent. Seeing God is dangerous enough, and one who survives such an experience is grateful (like Gideon; Judg 6:22). And yet the Penuel tradition, too, has managed to preserve traces of a physical struggle. The exact words that the writer uses for his etymology, "seeing [a] face," are ambiguous. Granted, the most basic meaning, the *peshat*, of "I have seen a divine being face to face" involves nothing more than *seeing*, but there existed another meaning in the context of war, to which the writer alludes. We find an example of this other meaning in 2 Kings 14:8–11: "Then Amaziah sent envoys to King Jehoash son of Jehoahaz son of Jehu of Israel, with this message: 'Come let us *confront each other* [lit., "see one another's face," *nitra'eh panim*]' . . . But Amaziah paid no heed; so King Jehoash of Israel advanced, and he and King Amaziah of Judah *confronted each other* [lit., "they saw each other's face"] at Beth-shemesh in Judah." We have already seen this technique of the biblical writers: by employing the equivocal expression, the writer managed to suggest that, while "seeing [a] face" did occur at Penuel, it was not a violent *confrontation* but only the patriarch's *seeing* God's face—itself an event of great danger.

If we back up ten verses to the story that covertly interpreted the name Mahanaim, we find that it also contained two covert etymologies of Penuel! The first, in a verse we have already discussed, shares a bit of the sense of the overt etymology ("see [another's] face") by mentioning the word "face" four times:

> And you shall say [to Esau], "And your servant Jacob himself is right behind us." For he thought, "If I make amends [lit., "cover his face"] with a gift that goes before me [lit., "to my face"] and only afterwards *look on his face*, perhaps he will show me favor [lit., "lift my face"]." (32:21)

The second was embedded into the story's continuation, into the meeting between Jacob and Esau. There the patriarch tells his brother: "No, pray, if I have found favor in your eyes, accept my gift from my hand, for *to see your face is like seeing the face of God [penei 'elohim]*" (33:10). This name explanation is more exact than the others since it includes both elements of the name Penuel, *panim*, "face," and *'el*, "God." Jacob's reference to seeing God's face, to which he likens seeing his brother's face, alludes to the offering one must make when one sees God (Exod 23:15; 34:20: "and none shall appear before Me [lit., "my face will not be seen"] empty-handed"). The writer who inserted this interpretation wanted to cancel any notion of Penuel's sanctity, as though to say: there was no *actual* seeing of God's face in that place but only a seeing that was *analogous* to it—it was "*like* seeing the face of God."

In the traditions swirling around Penuel, therefore, we have discovered a process similar to what occurred regarding Mahanaim. The overt name derivation—weakened as it is— admits to a meeting with a divine being (though denying any physical struggle), while the covert etymologies shifted the tradition from the realm of the holy to the profane: to the meeting between Jacob and Esau. And again, Jacob's fear of his meeting with Esau seems to preclude his having the courage to fight a divine being.

There is reason to ask: Why are the traditions about Penuel and Mahanaim so intertwined? These two cities on the banks of the Jabbok never coexisted as strong settlements. Instead, when the first thrived, the second's star fell. In the period of the judges, Penuel's prominence rose until it was destroyed by Gideon (Judg 8:17). At the beginning of the monarchic period, Mahanaim was the region's most important city, and it continued to be so until the conquests of Shishak, king of Egypt, at which point Penuel's influence reemerged, having been rebuilt by Jeroboam, the first king of the Kingdom of Israel (1 Kings 12:25). Thus, with the seesawing of the two, traditions that were associated with the destroyed city apparently became transferred to the other, which rose in its stead. Traditions wandered between Penuel and Mahanaim, even becoming fused together.

But it was not only cities along the Jabbok that claimed stories about a struggle between Jacob and an adversary. A similar tradition, which includes the element of the name change from Jacob to Israel, is associated with Bethel, a city that has already played an important role in Jacob's life. The tradition that locates the struggle in Bethel is found far from the hub of stories about Jacob in Genesis. Instead, it awaits us in Hosea 12, which we referred to in discussing the etymology of Jacob's name: "in the womb he deceived his brother . . ." (v 4). The next words of that verse read:

> In his vigor, he strove [*sarah*] with God ['*elohim*]. He dominated over an angel and prevailed. The other wept and implored him. At Bethel he met him and there he spoke with us

[the Septuagint preserves the correct reading, "with him"]. (vv 4–5)

The tradition strongly resembles that of the struggle/name change at Penuel: compare "For you have striven with God . . . and have prevailed" (32:29) with "he strove with God . . . and prevailed." What's more, in the middle of the struggle at the Jabbok, the divine entity turned to Jacob and requested, "Let me go, for dawn is breaking" (Gen 32:27), while in Hosea, he "wept and implored him."

Hosea's words twice interpret the name Israel: into the original etymology—"he strove with God and prevailed" (which is identical to what is told in Gen 32:30)—the words "He dominated [*vayasar*] *over* [*'el*] an angel" have been inserted. The purpose was to diminish the impact (if only slightly) of the story of Jacob's wrestling with God by reducing it to a meeting between the patriarch and an angel. The writer of the added words wrote under the influence of the tradition of the struggle at Penuel, where Jacob wrestled with the man = angel. The preposition *'el*, "over," was purposefully chosen here (*'el* and the more unambiguous *'al* were interchangeable for this sense in biblical Hebrew) in order to supply the second element in the name etymology, since it effectively removes "God" (*'el*; written identically but vocalized differently) from Jacob's new name.

Hosea 12:4–5 contains interpretations not only of the patriarch's two names, Jacob and Israel, but of two of the names of the cultic site in which the meeting occurred, with the place's third name—Bethel—being mentioned overtly. The first name covertly interpreted is Beth-on ("In his *vigor* [*uve'ono*] he strove with God"). The form of the name Beth-on (in which we hear the element *'on*, "power, vigor, manhood," i.e., "House of Vigor") is alluded to only in Hosea 12:4 and, in transliteration, in the Septuagint to Joshua 18:12; 1 Samuel 13:5; 14:23. In all other appearances of the name in the Hebrew Bible, the vocalization, albeit slight, was deliberately altered to the defamatory Beth-aven, "House of Iniquity."

The words "[he] wept [*bakhah*] and implored him" interpret Bokhim, a place-name that received a number of explanations in the Bible. It is twice connected with Jacob: in Hosea 12:5 and Genesis 35:8, a verse to which we will soon return. In Hosea, it is Jacob's adversary who weeps as he pleads for release. The adversary is first identified as God, but from the moment that the words "he dominated over an angel" appear, the reader is expected to understand that the one who cried was an angel. This tendency to switch the crier's identity becomes more conspicuous in the etymology of the name Bokhim in Judges 2:1–5, which took issue with the older Hosea tradition. Also, here God is replaced by an angel, though this angel neither begs nor cries before Jacob-Israel but rather reproves his descendants, the Israelites, for their persistent idol-worshiping. It is they who wail upon hearing his words: "An angel of the Lord came up from Gilgal to Bokhim [the Septuagint adds: to Bethel] . . . the people broke into *weeping*. So they named that place Bokhim . . ."

One more explanation that tried to erase any connection between the appearance of a divine entity and Bokhim appears in Judges 20–21, the story of the concubine of Gibeah. That story tells how the tribes of Israel were repeatedly defeated by the Benjaminites and retreated to Bethel each time, crying and lamenting to God:

> For the Israelites had gone up [the Septuagint adds: to Bethel] and wept before the Lord until the evening (20:23) . . . Then all the Israelites, all the army, went up and came to Bethel and they sat there, weeping before the Lord (v 26) . . . The people came to Bethel and sat there until the evening before God. They wailed and wept bitterly. (21:2)

Ripples from the tradition of the struggle and name change at Bethel can be found also in Genesis 35:9–15. The writer of these verses knew the tradition about a struggle and he, too, argued against it and sought to replace it with a meeting in which God appears to Jacob and blesses him: "God appeared again to Jacob on his arrival from Paddan-Aram, and He blessed him" (note the similarity with Gen 32:30). Jacob's name change is no longer explained by a physical struggle—"because you have striven [*sarita*]," "in his vigor he strove [*sarah*]"—but is derived from the word *melakhim*, "kings," a synonym of *sarim* (see Isa 49:7; Jer 17:25), which contains sounds similar to those in *yisra'el*:

> God said to him, "You whose name is Jacob, your name shall no longer *be called* Jacob, but Israel shall be your name," and He called his name Israel. And God said to him, "I am El Shaddai. Be fruitful and multiply. A nation, an assembly of nations shall descend from you, and kings shall issue from your loins." (vv 10–11)

Wanting to remove any hint of a struggle between Jacob and God, the passage in Genesis 35 insists that the meeting involved only God speaking to Jacob, a point made three times, forcing the reader to notice this controversial contention: "God parted from him at the spot where He *had spoken* to him" (v 13), "and Jacob set up a pillar at the site where He *had spoken* to him" (v 14), and "Jacob gave the site, where God *had spoken* to him, the name Bethel" (v 15). It is particularly interesting that Genesis 35's efforts to confuse the ancient tradition reflected in Hosea ultimately returned to Hosea, like a boomerang, where, in a secondary stage, the words "there he spoke with him" were added by a writer who sought—in the spirit of Genesis 35—to replace the physical struggle with an exchange of words.

Despite the Bible's various attempts to obscure the ancient

tradition of a physical confrontation at Bethel, it is clear that in the city itself, people continued to speak of it. The Bordeaux pilgrim, who arrived at Bethel in 333 c.e., kept a travel diary, the oldest extant record of a Christian pilgrim in the Land of Israel. There we find that Bethel "was the place in which Jacob had fallen asleep on his way to Mesopotamia . . . and he saw an angel and the angel wrestled him."

Another similarity between Hosea 12 and Genesis 35 is the juxtaposition they both create between the etymology of Bokhim and the story of the struggle. In Genesis 35, the watered-down tradition of the confrontation is preceded by a short episode about the death of Rebekah's wet nurse, who "was buried under Bethel under the oak; so it was named Alonbakhut [lit., "oak of weeping"]" (v 8). The episode insinuates that the place received its name in reference to the tears shed over the wet nurse's death. Whereas the etymology for Bokhim in Judges separated the name's significance from Jacob's life, the tradition in Genesis kept it there but changed its substance.

The Bible preserves one more etymological tradition concerning Jacob's new name, this time relating it to *yashar*, "honest, straightforward," the exact opposite of the original interpretation of Jacob's name. The interpretation that relates Israel to *yashar* is found in the prophet Balaam's blessing of the Israelites, in Numbers 23:10—"Who can count the dust of Jacob, who can count the dust-cloud of Israel? May I die the death of the *upright* [*yesharim*], May my fate be like theirs!"— and Micah 2:7, which used it to censure the Israelites: "The one who is said to be the House of Jacob [*he'amur beit ya'aqov*]—Is the Lord's patience short? Is such His practice? To be sure, My words are friendly to those who walk uprightly [*hayashar holekh*]." In addressing "the one who is said to be the House of Jacob," the prophet alludes to Genesis 32:29: "And he said, 'No longer Jacob shall your name *be said*, but Israel.'" Micah disagrees with what was written in Genesis and claims that Jacob's name must remain Jacob since the people are still cheaters and undeserving of the name Israel, the name that befits one "who walks uprightly."

One more prophet makes use of the Jacob-Israel name change: "Listen to this, O House of Jacob, who are called by the name Israel . . . Who swear by the name of the Lord and invoke the God of Israel, though not in truth and sincerity" (Isa 48:1). From his use of the root *q-r-'* (the root of *niqra'im*, "are called"), it is clear that this prophet (whom scholars call Deutero-Isaiah) was using the story of Jacob's name change in Genesis 35:10 ("You whose name is Jacob, your name shall no longer *be called* [*yiqare'*] Jacob"). Deutero-Isaiah addresses the nation with the name "House of Jacob" despite their "being called" Israel, because in their swearing and deceitful behavior, the name Jacob suits them best.

An effort to attach the meaning of *yashar* to Israel and root out the association of Jacob with deceit and cheating is also reflected in the creation of the name Yeshurun. The success of that name was limited, however, and it appears in only a few verses in Deuteronomy (32:15; 33:5, 26) and once in Deutero-Isaiah: "Thus said the Lord, your Maker, Your Creator who has helped you from the womb: Fear not, My servant Jacob, Yeshurun whom I have chosen" (Isa 44:2). In that verse, the prophet may have alluded to the story of Jacob's birth, saying that God chose Jacob, who is *yeshurun*, that is, the "honest, upright one," already in his mother's womb, proving that Jacob did not win his status through any act of deceit.

I have already mentioned how, in the story of the struggle at the Jabbok ford, Jacob received a blessing through force, not deceit. From the moment that Jacob returns to Canaan, he is like Israel, *yashar,* upright, and no longer Jacob the deceiver. Now, finally, we return to the story in Genesis and the scene of the meeting between the two brothers, Esau and Jacob.

Jacob leaves the Jabbok limping, exhilarated and enlivened

from his encounter with the divine being whom he defeated and whose blessing he received, and he is immediately thrown back into his apprehensions concerning the impending meeting with Esau. His messengers, we recall, had reported how Esau and his militia of four hundred men were fast approaching and now, suddenly, the unavoidable moment arrives: "Jacob looked up and saw and, behold, Esau was coming and, with him, four hundred men" (33:1). Jacob, who had fearfully divided his herds into two camps, now hurries to arrange his family, trying to minimize any risk: "He divided the children among Leah, Rachel, and the two maidservants. And he positioned the maidservants and their children first, and Leah and her children after them and Rachel and Joseph last" (vv 1–2). With this arrangement Jacob objectifies the sentiment he feels toward his various wives and children. The maidservants and their children are less important than Leah and her children; Rachel and her son, Joseph, are the most precious. We can only assume that this was obvious, too, to the women and children who saw how he was ready to endanger them for the sake of Rachel and Joseph's well-being.

Jacob gathers his courage: "And he passed before them and bowed to the ground seven times until he was near his brother" (v 3). This man, who stole the blessing that gave him command over his brothers ("Be master over your brothers, and let your mother's sons bow to you"; 27:29), now bows seven times before Esau to atone for his past transgressions. Perhaps it was this display of obeisance, or perhaps Esau's intentions were already peaceful and Jacob had misinterpreted things, wrongly viewing Esau as heading up a militia. In any case, Esau has forgiven his brother, his rage forgotten over the twenty years that have passed since they last saw one another: "And Esau ran towards him and embraced him and fell on his neck and kissed him, and they wept" (v 4).

The brothers burst into tears, their emotions at the long-overdue reunion overwhelming them. For Jacob at least, these must also have been tears of relief and release from tension. These two, who had last met as young men, now see themselves in one another and acknowledge the changes that have transpired. It is not only the lines on their faces that are now creased; each man brings with him knowledge earned through hard experience, experiences not shared by the other. Once the initial excitement has passed, Esau has a moment to notice Jacob's family: "And he lifted his eyes and he saw the women and the children and he said, 'Who are these with you?'" (v 5). Jacob answers humbly and with an offering of thanks to God: "The children with whom God has favored your servant," once more referring to himself as Esau's servant, as he did previously (32:19, 21). Now that the potential for danger is past, Jacob's family and household members approach Esau in the order determined by Jacob, and each bows low: "The maidservants came forward with their children and bowed. And Leah came forward, too, with her children and they bowed, and afterwards Joseph and Rachel came forward and bowed" (vv 6–7).

Esau's curiosity is not yet satisfied, however, and he asks about the gift Jacob had sent: "'What do you mean by all this camp that I have met?' And he said, 'To find favor in my lord's eyes'" (v 8). Esau initially refuses—"I have much. Let what is yours be yours" (v 9)—though it is hard to know whether this is genuine or mere politeness, the rules of negotiations. Perhaps, at first, Esau really did not intend to benefit from Jacob's property, since his wealth, too, was ample, as he tells Jacob and as is demonstrated by the private army that he commands. But Jacob does not relent: "No, pray, if I have found favor in your eyes, accept my gift from my hand, for to see your face is like seeing the face of God, and you received me" (v 10). The verse, we notice, preserves the covert name etymology of Penuel— "like seeing the face of God"—which cancels any notion of a struggle with God having taken place there, as well as the interpretation of Mahanaim as derived from *minḥah*, "my gift." One more covert interpretation of Mahanaim hides in verse 8, in Esau's question, "What do you mean by all this *camp* that I have met?"

Jacob continues: "Please take my blessing, which has been brought to you, for God has favored me and I have everything" (v 11). God favored Jacob with children and with great wealth. Acknowledging God's grace in his good fortune, he does not hesitate to share it. In verse 10, Jacob called the gift "my gift," but in verse 11 he calls it "my blessing," expressing his wish to return the blessing that he stole long ago. The midrash explains: "He told him, the blessing that you hate me for, here it is, given to you" (*Pesikta Rabbati* 13). After being urged, Esau accepts (v 11).

Esau wants to continue the journey together, but Jacob prefers independence:

> And he said to him, "My lord knows that the children are frail and the sheep and the cattle that are nursing are my burden; if they are driven hard a single day they will die. Let my lord go before his servant, and I, let me proceed slowly, at the pace of the cattle before me and at the pace of the children, until I come to my lord in Seir." (vv 13–14)

Does he still fear Esau? Esau, in any case, is unpersuaded— "And Esau said, 'Let me assign to you some of the people who are with me'" (v 15)—but Jacob politely refuses the extra protection: "And he said, 'Why have I found favor in the eyes of my lord?'" With these words the meeting comes to a close: "and Esau returned on that day on his path to Seir. And Jacob traveled to Succoth and he built for himself a house and for his cattle he made huts [*sukot*]—that is why he called the place Succoth" (vv 16–17).

Jacob doesn't follow his brother, and he doesn't keep his promise to visit Esau in Seir; instead, he turns northward to

Succoth (Deir Alla, in the heart of the Jordan Valley). It seems apparent that Jacob still harbors doubts about his brother's true intentions—though perhaps he is projecting his own deficiencies. In any event, the two will reunite only briefly, when they meet to bury their father (35:29).

The parting of the brothers and the settling of one in Seir and one in Canaan was evidently the consequence of the tensions between the two, a remnant of Jacob's early behavior. The genealogy of Esau in Genesis 36, however, conveys a different view, wherein the brothers' parting was necessitated by their ample wealth:

> And Esau took his wives and his sons and his daughters and all the members of his household and his livestock and all his cattle and all the goods that he had acquired in the land of Canaan, and he went to [the] land [of Seir (thus in the Peshitta)] away from Jacob, his brother. For their possessions were too great for them to dwell together and the land of their sojournings could not support them because of their livestock. And Esau settled in the hill country of Seir . . . (vv 6–8)

This tradition appears to have been modeled on the parting of Lot from Abraham, and on Abraham's having chosen to settle in the land on the other side of the Jordan:

> And also Lot, who went with Abraham, had flocks and herds and tents, and the land could not support them staying together; for their possessions were so great . . . and Lot chose for himself the whole plain of the Jordan, and Lot journeyed eastward, and they parted one from the other. Abraham dwelled in the land of Canaan and Lot dwelled in the cities of the plain, and he pitched his tent near Sodom. (Gen 13:5–12)

A similar version of a just division of property between Jacob and Esau, initiated by God, is reflected in Joshua's historical survey: " . . . And I gave Isaac Jacob and Esau. To Esau I gave the hill country of Seir as an inheritance, and Jacob and his sons went down to Egypt" (Josh 24:4), where no fraternal tensions remain.

Jacob's journey from Haran to the Land of Israel was not an easy one. The move was paved with mysterious conflicts that did—or did not—take place with "God and men" as well as a meeting with Esau, which ended happily, though preceded by great trepidation and fear. Who can tell what surprises still await our hero, whether he will find rest, and whether his past deeds will finally cease to haunt him.

7

"Should our sister be treated like a whore?": Jacob in Shechem

JACOB'S FIRST stop after crossing the Jordan and arriving in the Land of Canaan is in the outskirts of Shechem, the city that would become the political and religious heart of the Kingdom of Israel. Three traditions connecting Jacob's biography with Shechem appear in succession between the end of Genesis 33 and the beginning of chapter 35. A fourth, compact and startling, is tucked into Jacob's testament to his son Joseph at the end of the patriarch's life. Let us now examine these traditions, their meanings, and the nuances between them.

The verse that opens the story of Jacob's first encounter with Shechem introduces the city: "and Jacob came *shalem* to the city of Shechem that was in the land of Canaan when he came from Paddan-Aram, and he set up camp before the city" (Gen 33:18). I have kept the word *shalem* in transliteration since its appearance is problematic. What does it mean? One possible understanding is as the adverb "unharmed, safely," which would connect it with a story we have already read, about Jacob's oath in Bethel: "And Jacob made a vow, saying, 'If God is with me and protects me . . . and I return *safely* [*beshalom*] to my father's house, and the Lord will be my God" (28:20–21). Indeed, after the dangerous escape from his father-in-law and the no less precarious meeting with his brother, not to mention his surprise encounters with various divine beings, Jacob's safe arrival is significant. Perhaps it is the Bible's sense of irony, then, that the family's safety will now become threatened in Shechem? But let's not get ahead of ourselves.

Another possible understanding of *shalem* reads it as a place-name, Shalem, with "the city of Shechem" functioning as an appositive clause. This was how a number of ancient translators understood the verse (e.g., Septuagint, Peshitta, Vulgate). Eusebius, too, in his *Onomasticon*, identified Shechem and Shalem as two names for the same city. The Book of Jubilees preserves both interpretations of the word: "And in the first year of the sixth week he went up to Shalem, which is east of Shechem, safely" (30:1). It avoids, we note, an exact identification of Shalem with Shechem, preferring to assume that it is a place east of that city, the direction from which Jacob arrives.

The identification of Shalem with Shechem corresponds with Samaritan belief. The Samaritans believe in the supreme sanctity of Shechem and reject Jerusalem's holiness. They identify Shalem—where Abraham met Melchizedek, king of Shalem, recognized its sanctity, and extended a tithe of all he had to its king-priest (Gen 14:18–20)—in Shechem. Shalem is identified with Jerusalem in Psalm 76:2–3—"God has made Himself known in Judah, His name is great in Israel; Shalem became his abode; Zion, His den" (Zion is another name for Jerusalem)— but Psalms lies outside the Samaritan canon, which contains only the Torah, the Five Books of Moses.

In any case, Jacob wastes no time. He has only just arrived in Shechem when he buys land, "where he pitched his tent from the sons of Hamor, the father of Shechem, for a hundred kesitahs" (33:19). The parcel of land becomes sanctified by his next action: "And he set up there an altar, and he called it El-Elohei-Israel" (v 20). This land will become the burial place of Jacob's beloved son Joseph (Josh 24:32).

This rather compact story about Jacob's purchasing land in Shechem joins three other stories of land acquisitions in Canaan: in Hebron (the cave of Machpelah; Gen 23:8–20), Jerusalem (Araunah's threshing; 2 Sam 24:21–24 = 1 Chron 21:22–25), and Samaria (1 Kings 16:24). Each of the four stories centers on a different capital city of biblical Israel. Hebron and Jerusalem were capitals of the Kingdom of Judah (Hebron was David's first capital when he was still king of Judah, alone; Jerusalem was the capital of David's unified kingdom); Shechem and Samaria were capitals of the Kingdom of Israel (Shechem was the first capital of Israel following the division of the united kingdom; Samaria was the capital of Omri's dynasty, and continued to serve as the capital of the Northern Kingdom until its demise).

It's worth taking a moment to look at these stories. The tradition about buying land in the Kingdom of Judah reminds us of Abraham and the land he bought that would become the burial place of the patriarchs: Hebron's cave of Machpelah. The story of Araunah's threshing floor in Jerusalem deals with the founder of the royal line of Judah—David. This same pattern is evident in the traditions about the Kingdom of Israel: the story about Shechem tells of the patriarch Jacob, the subject of our biography, while the isolated verse about the purchase of Samaria speaks of Omri, the founder of the most important dynasty in the Northern Kingdom.

It is certainly no coincidence that the longer traditions tell of Judahite cities, while those about the capitals of the Kingdom of Israel were preserved only as brief notes. Judahite writers and editors were dominant in the Bible's formation.

The purpose of buying land was either for erecting an altar (Shechem and Jerusalem) or for preparing a burial (Hebron and Shechem, where Joseph's bones will be brought). Graves and altars mark a landscape, trigger emotional attachment, and provide evidence of the landowners' or their heirs' presence. The Rabbis understood the ideology behind these stories, as seen in a midrash about our verse:

> "the plot of land which he bought . . ." (Gen 33:19), Rabbi Yudan bar Simon said: This is one of the three places that the nations of the world cannot cheat Israel and say "they were seized by you through fraud." They are: the cave of Machpelah and the Temple and the grave of Joseph. (*Genesis Rabbah* 79:7)

The Bible also contains traditions about the conquest of three of the cities: Shechem (Gen 48:22), Hebron (Judg 1:10), and Jerusalem (2 Sam 5:6–8). The stories that tell of land purchases provide legitimacy for Israel's possession of them, with legal-polemic elements being preserved even in the short traditions from the Northern Kingdom. The Shechem episode identifies the price paid (one hundred kesitahs) and sellers' identities (the sons of Hamor) and mentions the altar being erected. The altar is even given a name, "El-Elohei-Israel," signifying the connection between the place and the God of Israel. Samaria is said to have been bought from Shemer for two talents of silver.

Abraham built his first altar in Shechem when he arrived in the Land of Israel after God's revelation to him there and His promise to give the land to his descendants (Gen 12:6–8). His next altar was erected in Bethel (v 8). Abraham's being credited with constructing altars in Shechem and Bethel, two places identified with Jacob, seems to have been done retroactively, under the influence of the Jacob stories, in order to solidify consensus around the sanctity of these two places not only among the inhabitants of Israel (who naturally identified with Jacob) but also with the inhabitants of Judah, who viewed Abraham as their authoritative ancestor and inspiration (see introduction). Moses, too, commands the Israelites to erect an altar in Shechem after crossing the Jordan and entering the Land of Israel (Deut 27:5–6), a command ultimately fulfilled by Joshua (Josh 8:30 ff.). This accumulation of traditions testifies to the importance and sanctity of Shechem within the circles in which these stories were created, and to the writers' desire to instill that value in the people's consciousness.

As long as Jacob and his household are camped outside Shechem and interaction between populations is limited to commercial transactions, relations remain peaceful. The mood changes dramatically in the next scene, however, when the boundaries between the various ethnic groups are broken. Dinah, Jacob's daughter, bored by having only brothers at home and not even one girlfriend with whom to share her thoughts, goes out "to see the daughters of the land." Perhaps, she thinks, she will find a soul-mate among them. But instead of being embraced by the female companionship that she seeks, Dinah finds herself the victim of the worst kind of male violence. Shechem, the son of Hamor, Hivite chief and leader of Shechem, sees her "and he lay with her and abused her." Immediately afterward, we read, he falls in love with his victim and wants to marry her. Of Dinah's thoughts, we (of course) hear nothing.

On learning of the atrocity, Dinah's father does nothing. Are we surprised at Jacob's response—or, more precisely, his lack thereof? Did Jacob think that, by marrying Shechem, Dinah should be satisfied? Or is it that he was privy to his sons' plans but the biblical author wished not to get him involved? In any event, Dinah's brothers are not willing to overlook their sister's violation and they decide to take revenge. While seemingly negotiating with Hamor and Shechem for their sister's hand in marriage, they stipulate that all male Shechemites must be circumcised. The Shechemites agree and fulfill their obligation, but while they are recovering from their wounds, weak and in pain, Dinah's brothers enter the city, kill all the men, and plunder their households. Dinah is freed by her brothers from the house of her rapist-kidnapper, yet once again we are told nothing of her thoughts or reactions to the violence around her. Dinah, the daughter and sister, is not the main figure in this drama from which nobody emerges unscathed. Shechem is revealed as a cruel rapist while Jacob seems indifferent to his daughter's suffering; the sons, albeit in defense of their family's honor, kill every last male in Shechem and plunder the city, acting with deception and bloodthirstiness.

How do we explain Dinah's story? How do we come to terms with such duplicity and violence, and with Jacob's paternal failure when confronted with his only daughter's suffering? The tale is truly puzzling. At this point we need to step back from the story into the world of scholarship since, especially in this case, some of the answers may be found there.

First of all, we note that the story somewhat resembles two others in Genesis where a female member of the patriarchal family is taken to the house of a foreign ruler who wishes to marry her, and is freed by God. Sarah is twice presented as Abraham's sister (when Abraham fears for his life) and taken to the royal palace (Pharaoh's and then that of Abimelech, the Philistine king of Gerar). In both stories, God intervenes and returns Sarah to her husband, and Abraham emerges with newfound wealth (Gen 12:10–20; 20). Rebekah is almost abducted by the men of Gerar (26:1–13). The similarities mustn't distract us, however, from the conspicuous difference with our story: the tales of the matriarchs end happily whereas the story about Dinah is stained with violence and bloodshed.

Why does our story take such a radically different direction from its predecessors? We are unable to answer these questions before we address a number of inconsistencies, four "rough spots" that are evidence of the story's complex and gradual composition. First, Shechem rapes and abuses Dinah (v 2), and only then falls in love and asks to marry her (v 3). Second, two of the references to Dinah's violation, in verses 13 and 27, occur in sentences that neither read smoothly nor fit well in their contexts. There are also blatant contradictions: for example, according to verse 13, Shechem alone was guilty of Dinah's defilement whereas in verse 27 the entire city is held responsible. These difficulties lead me to conclude that the abduction and rape were introduced into the story later and that other verses that continue this theme are also secondary (vv 5, 7b, 17, 26b).

Another problematic element is that the definition of Shechem's act toward Dinah as an "outrage [*nevalah*] . . . in Israel" (v 7) is anachronistic since "Israel" as a nation had yet to exist. This supports identifying the second part of verse 7 as a secondary addition.

And finally, according to verses 25–26, Simeon and Levi killed all the men of the city, after which they took their sister and left. But according to verse 27, all of Jacob's sons participated in the pillaging. In verse 30, however, Jacob complains only to Simeon and Levi, and they answer (v 31), as though the other brothers had not participated at all. This leads me to conjecture that the exclusive blame of Simeon and Levi was also a later addition.

It thus seems that Genesis 34, as we now have it, is not a monolithic text but a layered composition of multiple authorship. What's more, when we remove these secondary additions, the story looks very different:

> [1]And Dinah the daughter that Leah had borne to Jacob, went out to see the daughters of the land.[2]And Shechem son of Hamor the Hivite, chief of the land, saw her.[3]And his soul clung to Dinah daughter of Jacob and he loved the maiden

and he spoke to the maiden's heart.[4]And Shechem spoke to Hamor his father, saying, "Get me that girl for a wife."[6]And Hamor the father of Shechem went out to Jacob to speak with him.[7]And the sons of Jacob came from the field.[8]And Hamor spoke with them, saying, "Shechem my son longs for your daughter. Please give her to him as wife.[9]Intermarry with us—your daughters you will give us, and our daughters you will take for yourselves.[10]You will dwell among us and the land will be before you. Settle, move about, and acquire holdings in it."[11]And Shechem said to her father and to her brothers, "Let me find favor in your eyes and whatever you will say to me, I will give. Ask of me a bride-price ever so high, and gifts and I will pay what you tell me, only give me the young woman for a wife."[13]And the sons of Jacob answered Shechem and Hamor his father with deception and they spoke.[14]And they said to them, "We cannot do this thing, giving our sister to a man who has a foreskin, because it is a disgrace to us.[15] Only in this will we agree with you: If you will be like us, every male being circumcised.[16]And we will give our daughters to you, and your daughters we will take to us, and we will dwell with you and we will be one people."[18]And their words seemed good in Hamor's eyes and in the eyes of Shechem son of Hamor.[19]And the youth lost no time in doing the thing for he wanted Jacob's daughter and he was the most highly respected of all in his father's house.[20]And Hamor and Shechem his son came to the gate of their city and they spoke to the people of their city, saying,[21]"These people are in peace with us. Let them dwell in the land and move about it, for the land, behold, is ample before them; their daughters we will take for us as wives, and our daughters we will give to them;[22]Only this way will the men agree with us to dwell among us and to be as one people: that every male be circumcised as they are circumcised.[23]Their cattle and possessions and all their livestock, will they not be ours, if only we agree to them and they will dwell with us."[24]And all who went forth from the city-gate listened to Hamor and to Shechem his son and every male was circumcised, all who went forth from the city-gate.[25]And it came to pass on the third day, while they were in pain, and the sons of Jacob the brothers of Dinah each man took his sword and they came to the city unopposed and they killed every male;[26]Hamor and Shechem his son they killed by the sword.[27]The sons of Jacob came upon the slain and plundered the city.[28]Their flocks and their cattle and their donkeys, and what was in the city and what was in the fields, they took.[29]And all their wealth and all their children and their women they took captive, and all that was in the houses they plundered.

The first thing we notice is that in this, the original narrative, Dinah was not violated. Shechem simply fell in love and wished to marry her. Dinah's brothers, who disapproved, tricked and massacred the Shechemites. The verses that introduce rape and defilement into the story were apparently added to justify the brothers' violence.

The creator of this secondary layer did not dream up his ideas ex nihilo but was inspired by another story: that of Amnon and Tamar (2 Sam 13). There, too, we read of a man falling in love with the only daughter of the chief among the Hebrews, Tamar, daughter of David; the young lover is of the same noble family: Amnon, son of King David. And there the brother of the girl kills the lover after the latter placed full trust in him, when the drunken Amnon is killed on the command of his brother Absalom (who was Tamar's full brother) during the sheep-shearing festivities (13:26–29). Significantly, Amnon is killed out of revenge for having raped Tamar.

The interpolator in Genesis 34 perceived this fundamental similarity and, needing to justify Jacob's sons' brutality, added the rape to Dinah's story, further assimilating the one story to the other. In doing this, he borrowed the characterization of the rape as an "outrage *in Israel*," inadvertently introducing the anachronistic notion of a nation, "Israel," into the patriarchal stories. This proposal finds corroboration in the tight correspondence between the additions in verses 2 and 7 and certain verses from 2 Samuel 13:

Genesis 34	2 Samuel 13
and he lay with her and abused her (v 2)	And he abused her and lay with her. (v 14)
when they heard and were distressed and the men became very angry (v 7)	When King David heard . . . he became very angry (v 21)
because an outrage was done in Israel, . . . a thing not to be done (v 7)	Such things are not done in Israel! Don't do this outrage! (v 12; see also v 13)

What about the inconsistent attribution of blame, the added verses identifying only Simeon and Levi as guilty? In Genesis 49, Jacob, on his deathbed, will curse his three eldest sons, Reuben first and then Simeon and Levi:

> Simeon and Levi are a pair; Their weapons are tools of lawlessness. In their council let my person not be included, in their assembly let my presence not be counted. For when enraged they slaughtered men, at their pleasure they maimed oxen. Cursed be their rage so fierce, their wrath so ferocious! I will divide them in Jacob, scatter them in Israel. (vv 5–7)

Jacob's curses of his three eldest sons pave the way for his blessing of Judah, the chosen fourth son, but the circumstances that provoked the curses are not explained. Our interpolator's accusation of Simeon and Levi for the murders in Shechem was, apparently, a midrash, an explanation, of Jacob's deathbed curse (though the two do not correspond easily; see chapter 10). Genesis 34 along with Genesis 35:21–22, which describe

Reuben's transgression and explain his curse (we discuss this in the next chapter), cleared the stage for Judah to receive Jacob's blessing.

Let us turn now to briefly examine chapter 34 in its original form. The separation between the Canaanites and Jacob's family was broken by Dinah (Gen 34:1). Though she left to see the "daughters" and not the sons, it was enough to invite disaster. In any case, the fact that she wanted to visit with the "daughters of the land" is not necessarily promising: this term, *benot ha'arets*, appears only once more in the Bible, at the end of the frame story surrounding Jacob's stealing the blessing, when Rebekah voices her fears lest " . . . Jacob marries a Hittite woman [such as Esau had] from *the daughters of the land . . .*" (27:46).

As Dinah socializes with the local girls, "Shechem son of Hamor the Hivite, chief of the land" (v 2a), glimpses her. (The Hivites were descendants of Canaan [Gen 10:17], one of the Canaanite nations the Israelites meet when they return with Joshua to the land.) Seeing Dinah awakens Shechem's love and he wants to marry her (v 3), entreating his father to "get me that girl for a wife" (v 4). So far, it sounds like a sweet love story. The daughter of Jacob, a newcomer who has recently purchased land in the city's outskirts, is given the opportunity to marry the city's most desirable bachelor, the son of the chief of the land. Hamor approaches Jacob, whose sons, back from the fields, join in the negotiations. Hamor speaks first and makes a tempting offer (vv 8–10). Shechem and Dinah's marriage, Hamor declares, will be but the start of a complete and equal commingling between Jacob's people and the Hivites, a fusion that brings attractive economic possibilities and the opportunity, too, for the patriarchs to become permanent and equal inhabitants of the land. The young Shechem, love-stricken and inexperienced with negotiation strategy, is excited by the chance to win his beloved Dinah, the young (and beautiful?) exotic foreigner. Without first consulting his father, the love-dazzled youth rushes to express his willingness to give anything for the girl (vv 11–12).

We would have expected Jacob to answer Hamor's offer, but this passive father leaves the negotiations to his sons who, in both the ancient and modern Near East, are responsible for their sister's honor. The cunning brothers lie to Hamor and Shechem, setting a precondition that the people be circumcised (vv 13a, 14–16). The sons answer Shechem and his father "with deception [*bemirmah*]" (v 13), recalling Jacob's dupery in acquiring his father's blessing (Gen 27:35). Though Jacob has not entangled himself in any duplicitous acts since returning from Haran, his sons seem to have learned a chapter or two from him. In their deception of Hamor and Shechem, the brothers also pull the wool over the eyes of their father, who is ignorant of their scheme. Their stipulation that the Shechemites be circumcised does not sound preposterous to Jacob (or readers) since the foreskin's removal indeed played an important role in differentiating the Israelites from other nations (see, e.g., Josh 5:9; Judg 15:18; 1 Sam 17:36).

Hamor and Shechem accept the brothers' condition (v 18); indeed, Shechem's enthusiasm has not waned (v 19). Now, Hamor and Shechem must somehow persuade their countrymen that the benefits of circumcision will outweigh the physical pain they will suffer. The speeches they deliver to their townsmen are constructed for persuasion, downplaying any possible threats and highlighting the merits (vv 20–21), and the bitter pill—the need for circumcision (v 22)—is immediately candy-coated, with promises of "cattle and possessions" (v 23), which are not entirely accurate. Neither Hamor nor Shechem mentions the real purpose of their negotiations.

The Shechemites, blinded by the opportunity for great wealth, agree to their leaders' proposal (v 24) and all of Jacob's sons (this, I remind you, is the original story) kill the incapacitated men of Shechem in cold blood (vv 25–26a) and loot the town (vv 27a, 28–29). Hamor and Shechem had promised their countrymen that all of Jacob's and his sons' property would be theirs; now the brothers pillage the Hivites, taking all their valuables, women, and children.

More than once in the story of Jacob's life we have seen that acts of treachery and deceit do not remain unpunished, that accounts are settled. Jacob's sons' brutal deception will find its retribution hundreds of years later, in the time of Joshua. Joshua will be called on to kill the inhabitants of the land, but the Hivites will deceive him and his men by disguising themselves as foreigners so that Joshua and the Israelites seal a pact with them and do not include them in their massacre (Josh 9). The slaughter of the Hivites in our story is thus answered with their being preserved safe in the days of Joshua!

In its original form, Dinah's story looked askance at the course chosen by Jacob's sons, their acting "with deception" in order to prevent Dinah's marriage to an uncircumcised man. The interpolation, too, which attributed the actual massacre to Simeon and Levi, was aimed at disgracing the two brothers and justifying their father's curse in chapter 49. That said, a subsequent writer/interpolator later added verses 30–31, which reflect a different evaluation of the killing. Here Jacob is depicted negatively; his objections to the killing derive not from ethical concerns but fear: "You have brought trouble on me, making me odious among the inhabitants of the land, among Canaanite and Perizzite and I am few in number. And if they gather against me and attack me, I will be destroyed, I and my household" (v 30). And the sons respond, leaving Jacob speechless: "Should our sister be treated like a whore?" (v 31).

The about-face in verses 30–31 effectively—and at the very last moment—casts Simeon and Levi in a positive light. This viewpoint is continued in verse 5 of the next chapter: "As they [Jacob and his household] set out, a terror from God fell on the cities round about, so that they did not pursue the sons of Jacob." Jacob's family enjoyed the safekeeping of God, confirmation that God approved of the sons' actions.

Approval of Simeon and Levi's behavior in Shechem is also discernible in postbiblical literature. In the apocryphal Book of Judith, the eponymous heroine, who kills Holofernes, the commander of the invading Assyrian army, is a descendant of the tribe of Simeon (8:1). In the prayer she offers before making her way to the enemy camp, she summons the memory of the famous deed:

> O Lord God of my ancestor Simeon, to whom you gave a sword to take revenge on those strangers who had torn off a virgin's clothing to defile her, and exposed her thighs to put her to shame, and polluted her womb to disgrace her . . . so you gave up their rulers to be killed, and their bed, which was ashamed of the deceit they had practiced, was stained with blood, and you struck down slaves along with princes, and princes on their thrones. (9:2–3)

In Testaments of the Twelve Patriarchs, a book written in the second century b.c.e., in the Testament of Levi, we find the same tradition of a sword of divine origin delivered to those who would take revenge: "Then the angel brought me down to earth; and he gave me a shield and a sword and said, 'Take vengeance on Shechem because of Dinah, and I will be with you, for the Lord has sent me . . .'" (5:2–3; cf. Jubilees 30:17, 23).

From one complicated anti-Shechemite tradition to another: following the story of Dinah's rape in Shechem, Jacob is commanded to ascend to Bethel and erect an altar to the Lord (Gen 35).

> [1]And God said to Jacob, "Arise, go up to Bethel and sojourn there and make there an altar to the God who appeared to you on your flight from Esau your brother."[2]And Jacob said to his household and to all who were with him, "Put away

the alien gods in your midst, purify yourselves, and change your clothes.³Let us rise and go up to Bethel and I will make there an altar to the God who answered me on the day of my distress and who has been with me on the way I have gone."⁴They gave to Jacob all the alien gods that were in their hands and the rings that were in their ears and Jacob buried them under the terebinth that was near Shechem. . . . ⁶And Jacob came to Luz, that is Bethel, in the Land of Canaan, he and all the people that were with him.⁷He built there an altar and called the place El-Bethel, for there God was revealed to him on his flight from his brother.

Verses 1–4 are not altogether coherent, as this short episode contains polemical elements describing the removal of alien gods and their burial at Shechem (vv 2b, 4). Evidence for the elements' secondary nature is twofold:

a. Jacob is not commanded to remove alien gods but only to ascend to Bethel and build an altar there. The removal of the gods and their burial is presented, therefore, as deriving from Jacob's own initiative, and the members of his household obey his instructions before carrying out God's command.

b. Another part of Jacob's directive (the fulfillment of which is not reported) is entirely unrelated to the removal of the alien gods but rather addresses the preparations toward the anticipated meeting with the Holy: "purify yourselves and change your clothes" (v 2b), which we can compare to the Israelites' preparations before receiving the commandments at Mount Sinai, in Exodus 19:10, 14, and to the purification of the Levites in Numbers 8:7. There is no relation between purification and the removal of the idols.

The original wording of the episode can thus be reconstructed:

And God said to Jacob, "Arise, go up to Bethel and sojourn there and make there an altar to the God who appeared to you on your flight from Esau your brother" (v 1). And Jacob said to his household and to all who were with him (v 2a), "Purify yourselves and change your clothes (2bβ). Let us rise and go up to Bethel and I will make there an altar to the God who answered me on the day of my distress and who has been with me on the way I have gone" (v 3).

The interpolated verses, which speak about the burial of alien gods (identified in the exegetical literature as having been either the terafim Rachel stole from her father in Genesis 31:19 or the idols that Jacob's sons looted from Shechem), remind us of the tradition of the gathering of all the tribes of Israel in the temple at Shechem that takes place at the end of Joshua's life, when Joshua makes a covenant for the people (Josh 24). The two scenes bear a number of curious parallels:

a. The commands to remove the idols are almost identical: "Put away the alien gods in your midst" (Gen 35:2); "Put away the alien gods that you have among you" (Josh 24:23).

b. Both describe the placement of an item under the terebinth tree in Shechem: "They gave to Jacob all the alien gods that they had, and the rings that were in their ears, and Jacob buried them under the terebinth that was near Shechem" (Gen 35:4); "He (= Joshua) took a great stone and set it up under the *'alah* in the sacred precinct of the LORD" (Josh 24:26). The *'alah* in Shechem is, of course, the *'elah*, terebinth (and so it appears in the Septuagint). The deliberate alteration of the word's vowels in Joshua was an attempt to prevent a contradiction between Genesis 35 and Joshua 24: it would be impossible to imagine that a terebinth under which idols had been buried would be in the temple of the Lord and would have symbolized the covenant between God and Israel.

Once again, we find that anti-Shechemite sentiment hides behind the resemblance, which originated in the use made of

Joshua 24 by the writer of the additions in Genesis. That Judah-ite writer—who did not recognize Shechem's sanctity—found in Joshua 24 the materials for his own version about the tree that was in Shechem and what was buried under it. He added the verses in Genesis 35 in order to tell readers: that place in Shechem that you consider a legitimate temple of the Lord is not holy at all! It is impure! In point of fact, his verses insist, what *were* buried under the tree were idols that had been re-moved there by Jacob. It would have been unthinkable to con-sider as sacred a place where the remnants of idol worship were buried. This polemical nature was felt by the Greek translator of the Septuagint (or by the writer of the Hebrew version that lay before him), who added, at the very end of Genesis 35:4, "until this very day." These words removed the story from their immediate, one-time context and endowed it with endur-ing relevance: the place remains polluted until this very day.

This anti-Shechem tradition was later deployed by the Rabbis in the service of their polemic against the Samaritans, for whom Shechem is the most holy city:

> R. Ishmael son of R. Yossi went up to pray in Jerusalem. He passed a terebinth grove and was seen by a Samaritan who asked him, "Where are you going?" He said: "To go up to worship in Jerusalem." He said: "Would it not be better to pray at this blessed mountain than at that dunghill?" He said: "I will tell you what you resemble, a dog eager for car-rion. Because you know that idols are hidden beneath it, for it is written, 'And Jacob hid them,' therefore you are eager for it. . . ." (*Genesis Rabbah* 81:3)

In Genesis 35, the desire to defame Shechem became com-bined with the aim of glorifying Bethel, the place where God had wanted Jacob to build an altar and to worship Him. The story of building the altar in Bethel competes, therefore, with the construction of the altar in Shechem, which we found in

Genesis 33:18–20, and was meant to demonstrate God's preference for Bethel over Shechem.

The Rabbis viewed Shechem as the locale for a whole variety of evil deeds in biblical times, as a place generally characterized by wrongdoing. In the course of relating how Joseph was sent by his father to Shechem to check on his brothers' well-being, the midrash determined that "'he arrived to Shechem' (Gen 37:14), a place marked for wrong-doing. In Shechem they abused Dinah, in Shechem they sold Joseph, in Shechem was divided the kingdom of the House of David, 'Jeroboam fortified Shechem in the hill country of Ephraim . . . ' (1 Kings 12:25)" (*Tanḥuma, Vayeshev* 2).

One more tradition ties Jacob to Shechem. It appears in Jacob's words to Joseph in Egypt, following his promise that God will return his sons to the land of their forefathers: "And now, I assign to you *shechem*, one more than your brothers, which I wrested from the Amorites with my sword and bow" (48:22). There are those who have explained *shechem* in this verse not as a place-name but as a noun and thus avoid any conflict with Genesis 33:18 and its description of how Jacob *purchased* the parcel of land in Shechem. That is what we find in the Aramaic Targum Onkelos, "and I have given you one more portion than your brothers" (see also the Peshitta and Vulgate), and Rashi, among others, followed: "'Shechem,' meaning 'a portion.'" Although this definition of *shechem* has no strong confirmation in the Bible, perhaps an echo of such a meaning hides in the words of a psalm: " . . . I will *divide up* ['aḥalqah] Shechem" (Ps 60:8; 108:8)—perhaps an etymology of the name of the city using the root *ḥ-l-q*, which is synonymous with the root of *shechem*—and note also the close proximity between the words *ḥelqah* (portion) and the name Shechem in the tradition about the purchase of land in Shechem: "And he purchased the *portion* of land . . . from the sons of Hamor, Shechem's father . . ." (Gen 33:19; see also Josh 24:32).

However we understand *shechem* in verse 22, the tradition we find there is astonishing since we have never heard of Jacob conquering territories in Canaan using sword and bow! On the contrary, the Book of Genesis makes efforts to portray the patriarchs as men of peace, not conquerors. Genesis tells of the land being promised the patriarchs by God, and the promise is realized—the land is conquered—only after the return from Egypt, in the days of Joshua. Any disputes that arose between the patriarchs and their Canaanite neighbors were resolved peacefully (e.g., Gen 13:7–12; 21:25–32). The single violent episode involving a patriarch was Abraham's defeat of Chedorlaomer and the kings with him in order to rescue Lot and Lot's people from captivity (Gen 14:14–17). Readers who had difficulty with this contradiction between the patriarchs as men of peace and verse 22 solved it by claiming that it referred to Jacob, who helped his sons in their destruction of Shechem following the rape of Dinah. This is what we find in Targum Pseudo-Jonathan to Genesis 48:22: "And I have given you the city of Shechem, one more portion than your brothers, who have taken it from the Amorites when I came there. And I have risen and helped them with my sword and bow."

Attempts to harmonize Genesis 48:22 and the other traditions about Shechem were doomed to failure. This tradition, which promises the city of Shechem to Joseph (and Joseph is finally buried there; see Josh 24:32), is in fact an echo of some ancient tradition that told of the patriarchs fighting and conquering Canaanite territories. This tradition was rejected by the mainstream ideology reflected in Genesis, although it survived in this one verse.

Admittedly, when the Israelites follow Joshua into the land after their years of Egyptian bondage and wandering in the wilderness, force *is* used, but Joshua attributes the conquest to God and his miracles, and " . . . *not by your sword or by your bow*" (24:12). It is interesting that Joshua uses the exact same words, "sword [and] bow," as if deliberately speaking against the tradition of Genesis 48:22, against the notion of the patriarchs having captured the land by force. The fact that Joshua's speech takes place in Shechem strengthens this impression even more.

It is possible that the unique tradition about Jacob's conquering Shechem with sword and bow was the impetus for creating the tradition about the purchase of Shechem for a hundred kesitahs from the sons of Hamor, the father of Shechem (33:18–20), the first tradition we dealt with in this chapter. Perhaps the tradition in Genesis 48 is not the only surviving fragment of the tradition of Jacob as a war hero, a conqueror: the story about Jacob's struggle and victory over the man-angel may derive, ultimately, from the same stream as the tradition about the conquest of Shechem, an ideological-literary school that viewed Jacob as an all-powerful hero who wrestled "with God and with men" and vanquished all. In any case, the mainstream tradition has presented us with a very different characterization of our hero who, throughout the Shechem stories, demonstrates little aggression, let alone initiative.

8

"And Isaac breathed his last and died and was
gathered to his kin in ripe old age":
Deaths in the Family

As IF the hardships Jacob faced in Shechem were not
enough, more would come. As the family makes its way from
Bethel to Ephrath, the unimaginable suddenly occurs: Rachel,
Jacob's beloved, dies while giving birth to Benjamin, her second son (Gen 35:16–20). Rachel's birth pains increase on the
journey from Bethel (v 16) and the midwife tries to instill confidence: "Have no fear, for it is another boy for you" (v 17).
These words are enough to remind us of the demand Rachel
made to her husband back in chapter 30 when envy of her sister
Leah and Leah's fertility had gotten the best of her: "Give me
sons or I shall die" (v 1). The Sages did not miss the link between these two verses and interpreted Rachel's initial demand
as an inadvertent prophecy: "What had caused her to say, 'Give
me sons,' except that she was prophesying that she would die
prematurely . . ." (*Aggadat Bereshit* 52). And truly, the biblical
writer alludes to the fact that, with her demand, Rachel sen-

tenced herself to death. That she indeed intended sons in her demand is also apparent from the second etymology she adjoined to the name of her firstborn, Joseph: "May the Lord add another son for me" (30:24). Now, most ironically, Rachel dies with the fulfillment of that wish.

But she was not the only contributor to her early death. Jacob's response to Laban after Laban accused him of stealing the terafim—"With whomever you will find your gods, that person shall not live" (31:32)—proves to have been fateful too. The midrash commented: "'With whomever you find your gods, that person shall not live'—It was like a verbal slip of a ruler [which nevertheless was binding and brought terrible results]" (*Genesis Rabbah* 74:32).

And perhaps there was a further factor in Rachel's death: when he readied his household for the approaching reunion with Esau, we recall, the apprehensive Jacob singled out Rachel and Joseph and positioned them in the back row behind the maidservants Zilpah and Bilhah and their sons, and behind Leah and her sons, in order to shield them from harm. For this act of favoritism Jacob is now punished with the death of Rachel, and later with Joseph's disappearance.

Sensing her impending death, Rachel hurries to give the newborn child a name, "Ben-oni" (v 18). It is no coincidence that Rachel's foreboding, kindled following the family's departure from Bethel, resulted in the bestowal of this name. We have already mentioned Beth-on, one of the names given to the cultic site that was in Bethel. In that context we also referred to the prophet Hosea's interpretation of the place-name: " . . . in his vigor [*uve'ono*] he strove with God" (12:4). What I did not mention there is that the word *'on* carries two meanings in biblical Hebrew. The first refers to strength, virility, as in Jacob's words to Reuben: "you are my first-born, my might and the beginning of my vigor" (Gen 49:3). The second has to do with grief and weeping: "I have not eaten *in my mourning* [*be'oni*] . . . and have not given any of it to the dead" (Deut 26:14). The name Beth-on can thus be understood also as "House of Grieving," similar to the other name of Bethel's cultic site, Bokhim ("weeping"; see chapter 6). With her departure from Bethel/Beth-on (a city that will be included in the territory of the tribe of Benjamin [see Josh 18:22; 1 Chron 7:28]), and with her approaching death, Rachel gives her newborn son a name that expresses the extent of her sorrow: Ben-oni, "son of my sorrow."

The prophet Jeremiah, who created a midrash around the story of Rachel's death and the birth of Benjamin in his prophecy about the return of the exiled tribes, was aware of the connection between the name of the son and Rachel's weeping, and he developed that image in his famous words:

> Thus said the Lord: "A cry is heard on high, wailing, bitter weeping, Rachel weeping for her children, she refuses to be comforted for her sons, who are gone." Thus said the Lord: "Restrain your voice from weeping, your eyes from shedding tears; for there is reward for your labor," declares the Lord: "they shall return from the enemy's land. And there is hope for your future," declares the Lord: "Your sons shall return to their country." (Jer 31:15–17)

Jacob was aware of the sorrowful burden implied by the name Ben-oni and feared the fate that awaited the boy who carried such a name (we find a similar thought expressed by Jabets, who feared the name his mother had given him; see 1 Chron 4:9–10). Jacob, honoring his wife and his love for her, did not dare change the name in any extreme way: "and his father called him Benjamin [*binyamin*]" (Gen 35:18). Jacob tried to reinforce the positive sense of *'on* as related to "strength" and "vitality" by replacing it with *yamin*, "right," which also means "strength" (see Exod 15:6).

And now to the location of Rachel's grave. Did Rachel die

in Benjaminite territory close to Bethel, in Beth-on, as the mother's name for her son suggests? Or perhaps it was close to Bethlehem, the city of David's birth, in the territory of Judah? The verse that relates Rachel's death and burial—"And Rachel died and was buried on the road to Ephrath, that is Bethlehem. And Jacob set up a pillar on her grave, it is the pillar of Rachel's grave to this day" (35:19–20)—lends credence to the second possibility, and is joined, in this regard, by Jacob's remembrance of that melancholy day years later when, in Egypt, Joseph presents his sons Ephraim and Manasseh to his father: "And I, when I was coming from Paddan, Rachel died to my sorrow in the land of Canaan on the way, still some distance from Ephrath, and I buried her there on the way to Ephrath— that is Bethlehem" (48:7). The Bordeaux pilgrim (whom I mentioned in chapter 6), whose travel diary is the earliest extant record of a traveler to the Holy Land, reported on his visit to Rachel's grave in that same region: "From Jerusalem you arrive to Bethlehem in four miles. On the road on the right side, there is the pillar, that is where Rachel Jacob's wife is buried."

At odds with the tradition about Rachel's burial near Bethlehem in Judah is another that offers an alternate account of Rachel's burial in the territory of Benjamin. After the prophet Samuel anointed Saul (a Benjaminite) as Israel's first king, he informed Saul of a series of signs that would occur on Saul's return home that would testify that God was "with him." The first of these was that "when you leave me today, you will meet two men near the tomb of Rachel in the territory of Benjamin, at Tseltsah, and they will tell you that the asses you set out to look for have been found . . ." (1 Sam 10:2). Tseltsah is mentioned nowhere else in the Bible, but the verse states explicitly that Rachel's tomb is in the territory of Benjamin, placing it nowhere near Bethlehem and making it impossible to coordinate the two traditions, one about Judah and the other about Benjamin. The Rabbis felt this contradiction and solved it thus:

"How is it that we find that Rachel is buried in the territory of Benjamin, at Tseltsaḥ? And yet she was buried in Bethlehem, in the territory of Judah! . . . but [Samuel] told [Saul]: 'Now, as I speak with you, they are at Rachel's tomb. You will go and they are coming and they will find you in the territory of Benjamin, at Tseltsaḥ'" (*Tosefta Sota* 11.13). Let us try to understand these exegetical gymnastics: the two men, Samuel told Saul, who were now next to Rachel's tomb in Bethlehem (in the territory of Judah), would meet up later with Saul in the territory of Benjamin. Another tactic taken elsewhere by the Sages was to reverse the order of the words so that now Samuel tells Saul, "When you leave me today near the tomb of Rachel [i.e., from Bethlehem!], you will meet two men in the territory of Benjamin at Tseltsaḥ" (*Genesis Rabbah* 82:9). These efforts by the Rabbis only highlight the essential contradiction that exists in the biblical text.

Another verse relevant to our discussion tells of the burial of Saul, the Benjaminite king: "And they buried the bones of Saul and of his son Jonathan in Tsela [*tsela'*] in the territory of Benjamin, in the tomb of his father Kish . . ." (2 Sam 21:14). This verse appears to refer to a family grave. Is it possible that these two places, Tseltsaḥ and *Tsela'*, whose names bear both graphic and aural similarity, were, in fact, one and the same? If so, then the grave of Rachel, the matriarch of the Benjaminites, is also that of the preeminent Benjaminite family, that of King Saul.

The tradition of Rachel's having been buried in the territory of Benjamin also finds support in the prophecy of Jeremiah about the future return of the exiled, discussed above. Let's return to that prophecy, "A cry is heard on high . . ." (Jer 31:15). The word *beramah*, here translated as "on high," was translated in the Septuagint and Peshitta as though it referred to the name of a place, "in Ramah," Ramah being a city in the territory of Benjamin (see Josh 18:25; Neh 11:13). According to this tradition, Rachel died and was buried in a Benjaminite city, a view shared, despite the verse in Genesis, by the early sage Rabbi Meir, who stated that "she died [and therefore was buried, as per Gen. 35:19] in the portion of her son Benjamin" (*Sifre Deuteronomy* 352).

In the end, not surprisingly, the controversy around the location of Rachel's gravesite—whether in Benjamin or Judah— proves to have been political in nature: the tribe of Benjamin and the royal family that descended from Benjamin (the House of Saul) claimed Rachel for themselves, while the tribe of Judah and the dynasty descended from that patriarch (the House of David) made a similar—if opposing—claim. It may well be that the historical connection between these two tribes, stemming from their common experience under the Davidic dynasty in the Kingdom of Judah, stimulated the story about Bethlehem, which was meant to supplant the older tradition that told of Benjamin's mother's burial in his own territory, the territory of the tribe of Saul (and perhaps even in the same spot where King Saul was buried), and instead transferred it to the city of David's birth. The aim of the transfer was to reinforce ties between the two tribes, to establish the tribe of Benjamin's allegiance to the House of David, and secure it into an unbreakable bond.

The birth of Benjamin and death of Rachel signals an end to the childbearing chapter in Jacob's household. Now a "full count" of Jacob's progeny can be rendered. Indeed, such an account was attached to the story of the matriarch's death, in verses 22b–26, though they are now separated by a cursory report of a shocking occurrence in the patriarch's house: "And Israel journeyed and pitched his tent beyond Migdal-Eder. And it happened, while Israel stayed in that land, that Reuben went and lay with Bilhah, his father's concubine, and Israel heard" (vv 21–22a).

There is reason for the juxtaposition of the story of Reuben and his father's concubine with that of Rachel's death and, consequently, the interruption between Benjamin's birth and the genealogy of Jacob's descendants. Against the background of the favoritism Rachel regularly enjoyed at Leah's expense, Reuben, Leah's firstborn and jealous protector, sets out, immediately following the death of his mother's rival, in an attempt to dissolve all remaining ties between his father and the memory of the favorite wife by contaminating Bilhah, Rachel's maidservant and Jacob's concubine. The death of Rachel and defilement of Bilhah would leave Leah to become the family's matriarch with none to challenge that status. Jacob's intimate relations would be limited to Leah and Leah's maidservant, Zilpah. Reuben's motivation, according to the midrash, was clear:

> He sought his mother's revenge, since, for all the days that Rachel lived, her bed was near the bed of our father Jacob. When Rachel died, our father Jacob took Bilhah's bed and placed it near his bed. [Reuben] said: Is it not enough that my mother was jealous of her sister during her lifetime, but even after her death? (*Genesis Rabbah* 98:4)

This, then, was what propelled Reuben to do what he did. Defiling Bilhah guaranteed that Jacob would no longer visit her bed, similar to what is said about Absalom, son of David, who rebelled against his father and lay with David's concubines in order to strengthen his own position (2 Sam 16:21–22). David managed to suppress that rebellion, but he no longer had relations with the concubines (2 Sam 20:3).

Stories about a son having sexual relations with his father's concubine for the sake of his mother's honor are not unique to Israel's literature. One famous example is in the *Iliad*, where we read how Phoenix lay with his father's concubine, in compliance with his mother's wish:

> [I was then] fleeing from strife with my father Amyntor, son of Ormenus; for he was enraged with me because of his fair-

haired concubine, whom he himself ever loved, and scorned
his wife, my mother. So she begged me by my knees contin-
ually, to sleep with his concubine first myself, so that the old
man might be hateful in her eyes. I obeyed her and did the
deed, but my father learned of this immediately and cursed
me mightily, and invoked the dire Erinyes, that he should
never set on his knees a dear child begotten by me; and the
gods fulfilled his curse, Zeus of the nether world and dread
Persephone. (9.448–457; trans. A. T. Murray; Loeb Classi-
cal Library 1999)

As we know, Reuben has had a history of interfering in his
father's marital bed in order to further his mother's best inter-
ests. It was Reuben, we recall, who brought mandrakes to his
mother out of a belief in their powers to awaken sexual desire
(Gen 30:14–18). Note how, in both accounts, the description
of Reuben's activities includes the words "And Reuben went"
(30:14; 35:22). It goes without saying that, this time, Reuben's
action is immeasurably graver than the last.

The terseness of the Reuben and Bilhah story leads us to
suspect that the storyteller was trying to quickly end the em-
barrassing account. The episode received more lengthy coverage in two extrabiblical books, Testaments of the Twelve
Patriarchs and Jubilees. It may very well be that the longer versions we find in those two books in fact preserve elements from
a prebiblical tradition but which the biblical writer preferred to
omit or at least abbreviate.

In the Testament of Reuben, the first of the twelve, Reuben confesses his transgression to his sons, with the command
to learn from his errors:

... For had I not seen Bilhah bathing in a secluded place I
would not have fallen into so great a sin. ... For while our
father Jacob was away on a visit to his father Isaac, when
we were in Eder, near the house of Ephrath (*that is* Bethlehem), Bilhah had been drinking; and she was lying asleep

in her bedroom with nothing over her. And I went in and saw her nakedness and did the wicked deed; and I left her still asleep and went away. And immediately an angel of God told my father Jacob about my wickedness; and he came and mourned over me. And *as for Bilhah*, he had no further relations with her. (3:9–15)

In this expansion of the biblical story, the author of Testaments (or of the oral tradition that he knew) used well-known motifs: Bilhah's drunkenness could be borrowed from the story of Noah and his son Ham (Gen 9:20–27) or from the story of Lot's daughters (19:30–37). Bilhah's drunkenness, we observe, transfers some of the responsibility for Reuben's actions to her. The writer of the Testament also takes pains to explain the circumstances that allowed Reuben to lie with Bilhah: he re-orders events and specifies how Jacob had left to visit Isaac, a detail which, in Genesis 35, appears only after the genealogical list (v 27). The writer also clarifies how Jacob heard of Reuben's deed—"immediately an angel of God told my father"—as well as Jacob's reaction: "and he . . . mourned over me . . ."

The event receives an even longer retelling in the Book of Jubilees:

And Jacob moved and settled to the south of Migdal-Eder-Ephrata. And he went to *visit* his father Isaac, he and his wife Leah, on the new moon of the tenth month. And Reuben saw Bilhah, Rachel's maid, his father's concubine, bathing in water in a secluded place, and he became enamored of her. And he hid himself and went into Bilhah's house at night and found her asleep alone on her bed in her house; and he lay with her. And she woke up and looked round, and behold Reuben was lying with her on the bed; and she lifted the edge of her coverlet and took hold of him, and when she realized it was Reuben she cried out aloud. And she was ashamed because of him, and she let go of him and he fled. And she was much upset by what had happened and said nothing to any one about it. And when Jacob returned and asked for her, she said to him, "I am not clean for you, for I have been defiled: Reuben defiled me and lay with me in the night, when I was asleep, and I did not realize *who it was* until he had uncovered my shame and had intercourse with me." And Jacob was very angry with Reuben because he had lain with Bilhah—because he had uncovered his father's shame. And Jacob did not approach her again because Reuben had defiled her . . . (33:1–10)

The close relationship between this version in Jubilees and the account in Testaments is apparent. Reuben sees Bilhah bathing—an element influenced by the story of David's glimpse of the bathing Batsheva (2 Sam 11). Though Bilhah seems to be a passive participant in the Bible's version, the writer of Jubilees (in contrast to Testaments) takes pains to explicitly clear her of any suspicions: she bathes in a secluded place and is unaware of Reuben entering her bed; when she discovers Reuben's act she is distressed and confesses her defilement to Jacob, so that he learns of the deed from her. According to Jubilees, Jacob is furious with Reuben, and what we inferred from the juxtaposition of this story with that of Rachel's death and from the similarity of the story with Absalom and his father's concubines is now stated explicitly: Jacob never again had relations with Bilhah.

The writer of Jubilees, who routinely retold biblical stories in such a way that they were seen to have led to the establishment of specific laws, here alludes to both Leviticus 18:8 ("Do not uncover the nakedness of your father's wife") and Leviticus 20:11 ("If a man lies with his father's wife, it is the nakedness of his father that he has uncovered; the two shall be put to death . . ."), as well as to Deuteronomy 27:20 ("Cursed be he who lies with his father's wife . . .").

The thumbnail story of Reuben and Bilhah in Genesis is followed by a midverse break, that is, a space of a few letters that has been left empty in the Hebrew text between it and the next words, "Now the sons of Jacob were twelve in number . . ." Does this space preserve evidence that Jacob's response has been erased? In the Septuagint, for instance, following "and Israel heard," we find the words "and it was evil to him," which depict Jacob as responding with obvious bitterness to his son's behavior, though no verbal or physical expression of the rancor is described. His reaction is similar in Jubilees: "And Jacob was very angry with Reuben . . ."

The biblical editor seems to have deliberately left Jacob's response here incomplete, but it will come—forcefully and un-ambiguously—before our story ends, with Jacob's curse of his eldest son from his deathbed, in Genesis 49:3–4: "Reuben . . . you shall excel no longer, for when you mounted your father's bed, you defiled my couch, you mounted!" This, along with the curses of Simeon and Levi in the next verses, forms the first three parts of the three-four pattern that leads to the ultimate blessing of Judah. The incorporation of the tradition about Reuben and Bilhah in Genesis 35 (like the verses about Simeon and Levi that were added to the Dinah story in chapter 34) was therefore intended as an explanation for the curses against these tribes in Genesis 49. The relationship between Reuben's deed and the curse will be discussed in full below, in chapter 10.

The genealogy of Jacob's sons that now follows lists them in the order of their birth by mother: first the two wives (Leah first, since she mothered children before Rachel), then the two concubines (Bilhah first, since she became a mother before Zilpah).

> The sons of Leah: Reuben, Jacob's first-born, Simeon, Levi, Judah, Issachar, and Zebulun. The sons of Rachel: Joseph and Benjamin. The sons of Bilhah, Rachel's maid-servant: Dan and Naphtali. And the sons of Zilpah, Leah's maid-servant: Gad and Asher. These are the sons of Jacob who were born to him in Paddan-Aram. (Gen 35:23–26)

The author, we note, took pains not only to list Reuben first but to explicitly remind readers that he is "Jacob's first-born." (The genealogy's closing statement, that the sons had all been born in Paddan-Aram, is incorrect with regard to Benjamin, who was born on the return to Israel.)

The writer of Chronicles realized the implicit meaning behind the insertion of the Reuben and Bilhah tradition between the birth of Jacob's last son and the genealogy. The Chronicler, who possessed the broader perspective of the Book of Genesis and knew the destinies of the brothers/tribes, and particularly the principal roles that Joseph and Judah and their tribes would play, began his account of Reuben's line with an explanation: "The sons of Reuben the first-born of Israel. He was the first-born, but when he defiled his father's couch, his birthright was given to the sons of Joseph son of Israel, though he [Joseph] is not reckoned as first-born in the genealogy. Though Judah became more powerful than his brothers and a leader came from him, yet the birthright belonged to Joseph. The sons of Reuben, Israel's first-born of Israel: Enoch, Pallu, Hezron, and Carmi . . ." (1 Chron 5:1–3).

Reuben's violation of Bilhah, the Chronicler confirms, was what lost him the birthright. It may even be that the Chronicler considered Joseph as having inherited Reuben's birthright since—like the firstborn's double portion (Deut 21:17)—his portion of his father's inheritance was also doubled, in that his two sons, Manasseh and Ephraim, were numbered among the twelve tribes (see below, chapter 9).

Although he relinquished his rights as firstborn, Reuben continued to occupy the primary position in terms of pedigree. In this way Chronicles explained how, despite Reuben's having lost his firstborn rights, he is nonetheless explicitly identified as firstborn both in Genesis 35:23 and 49:3. The Chronicler's familiarity both with the Joseph stories, in which Judah plays the central role at the expense of the marginalized Reuben, and with Genesis 49, which elevates Judah to the status of ruler, caused him to place Judah at the very center: "Judah became more powerful than his brothers and a leader came from him."

Immediately following the genealogy, Genesis 35 proceeds to recount Jacob's return to his father's home: "And Jacob came to his father Isaac at Mamre at Kiriath-arba—that is Hebron—where Abraham and Isaac had sojourned" (v 27). The Bible observes the return of the long-lost son quietly and without fanfare. Verses 28–29 quickly report Isaac's death, and Rebekah is not mentioned at all, leading us to wonder whether she died prior to her beloved son's homecoming. This would represent a natural continuation of the unfulfilled hopes she whispered into Jacob's ears before sending him to Haran, that he would need to stay with Laban only a "few days" (27:44).

Although Rebekah's expectation was disappointed, other things she voiced prove to have been inadvertent prophecies. When her sons struggled within her, she had said, rather elliptically, "If so, why am I?" though the Peshitta has preserved the more comprehensible "Why am I alive?" leading us to wonder whether perhaps the word "alive" was omitted by a copyist who did not wish to depict Rebekah as pronouncing words that might represent a death spell. Whatever the case, Rebekah's suffering did not end with the birth of her sons. After Esau's marriage to a Canaanite woman, she expressed the same sentiment to Isaac: "If Jacob marries a Hittite woman like these from the daughters of the land, why do I live?" (27:46). This mother, it seems, who has twice pronounced death preferable to life, does not live to see her beloved son again before she dies, to see how tensions between the brothers subsided and how they made peace with one another. Rebekah's absence from the stage—and from life—when Jacob returns and when Jacob and Esau resume a relationship is not only God's covert response to her having tempted fate with her death wish but her punishment for the role she played, those many years ago, in stealing the blessing intended for Esau.

Ironically, it is Isaac who greets Jacob on his return: Isaac who was old and blind already before Jacob left for his extended exile, who had even expressed fear that he would soon die (Gen 27:1–4). The Bible has chosen to say nothing of the reunion between father and son or of emotions either felt. Instead, it preserves a verbose report of Isaac's death: "And the days of Isaac were one hundred and eighty years. And Isaac breathed his last and died and was gathered to his kin in ripe old age, and Esau and Jacob his sons buried him" (vv 28–29). Isaac was sixty when Esau and Jacob were born (25:26), and he lived another hundred and twenty years during their lives. Yet the number of scenes in which Isaac and his sons share the stage are remarkably few; all we read about their relations is that Isaac was partial to the older son, Esau, "because he had a taste for game" (25:28), and that he intended to bless Esau, who fed him game, and the consequences (27:1–28:9).

Esau and Jacob bury their father together. Does the writer's listing them according to their birth order (cf. Isaac and Ishmael's mention in Gen 25:7–9) perhaps represent a covert protest against all that Jacob did in order to secure the birthright and its many benefits? Or perhaps Esau is listed first to remind us that Esau was Isaac's favorite, and that Esau succeeds in burying his father while the other son, the favorite of the mother, was not present at *her* burial. I don't have an answer to these questions, but the close parallel with the description of Abraham's burial (Gen 25:7–9) leads us to believe that the order was deliberate. In any case, the two brothers share in the burial of their father and they seem at ease with one another, as were Ishmael and Isaac when they buried their father.

Jacob's homecoming was thus filled with hardships. The rape of his daughter Dinah, the death of his beloved wife, intimate relations between his firstborn and his concubine, the long-awaited reunion with his mother that did not occur, and, finally, the death of his father (though, it must be admitted, Isaac died after a long life) comprise a chain of dramatic and difficult events. Jacob, it seems, continues to pay for the wrongs he committed in his youth, and with high interest. The transgressions of his past continue to dog him; unfortunately, his burden of sorrows has—even now—yet to be filled.

9

*"And Israel loved Joseph more than all his sons,
for he was the son of his old age":
Priority of the Young*

THERE COMES a time when a person must make room for
the next generation; pushed off center stage, you suddenly become the "father of . . ." or "mother of . . ." And indeed, with
the rising of Joseph's sun, Jacob's begins to slowly set. Genesis 37:2, "This is the line of Jacob: Joseph was seventeen years
old . . . ," signals this hegemonic transition, the opening of
Joseph's biography, which continues (with light interruption)
till the very end of the Book of Genesis and reserves only a
secondary role for Jacob. The literary quality of Joseph's story
differs from Jacob's. We can characterize it as a long novella
of many scenes and plots that portray the primary figure, Joseph, as developing and changing. Even the figure of God has
changed within Joseph's biography: the story's restful rhythm
does not make any direct or explicit actions of God necessary.
God accompanies and gently guides the central figure using
invisible threads—"and all that [Joseph] did the Lord made

succeed" (39:3)—but the center of the stage, for better or for worse, is occupied by humans.

Despite the changed tone, there is decided continuity: it would be impossible to fully comprehend the characters in the Joseph narrative apart from Jacob's stories. It will soon become apparent, too, that Jacob's stories cast a long shadow over Joseph's, with accounts opened during the Jacob cycle finally closing in the course of his son's biography. Joseph, whom we first met fleetingly at his birth (30:23) and then caught a quick glimpse of just before the meeting with Esau (Gen 32:2), is now "seventeen years old . . . tending the flock with his brothers, and he was a helper to the sons of Bilhah and the sons of Zilpah, his father's wives" (37:2). The storyteller does not explain how it is that the son of Jacob's favorite wife has been relegated to such a subordinate position, to serving the sons of concubines. One can imagine that it was Leah's sons who sought to demean him out of a jealous protection of their mother (a jealousy that led, we recall, to the firstborn Reuben's having relations with Bilhah)—particularly since both Leah's sons and those of the two concubines have certainly not forgotten how, when the family faced danger, their father used them to shield Joseph and his mother (32:2). It is thus not inconceivable that the concubines' sons treated Joseph cruelly or that he, having yet to learn self-restraint, brought "a bad report of them to their father" (37:2), thereby contributing, himself, to their resentfulness. The narrator tells us nothing of Jacob's response to his younger son's tattling. If we can judge from Jacob's general disposition until now, he did nothing—he certainly didn't chastise Joseph. In fact, in the story's very next words we read: "And Israel loved Joseph more than all his sons, for he was the son of his old age" (v 3). Jacob, it turns out, has learned nothing from his experiences! Having experienced the cost of a parent's favoritism, he now repeats his own parents' mistake. Jacob, whose mother loved him best and favored him though he was the youngest, now brims with excess love for his young son, Joseph.

And that is not all. The biblical writer next gives an example of Jacob's preferential treatment: "and he made him an ornamented tunic" (v 3). As we have consistently seen throughout our study of Jacob's life, every detail the biblical narrator chooses to relate is significant. Like the Chekhovian directive of narrative efficiency that warns us to beware of the gun hanging on the wall in a drama's first scene, the colorful tunic that Joseph receives from his father will—predictably—play a crucial role in the dramatic events to come. It is Joseph's father's love for him that awakens the brothers' fierce jealousy and hatred: "And his brothers saw that their father loved him more than his brothers and they *hated* him and could not speak a friendly word to him" (v 4). Back in chapter 29, Leah had been the "hated" wife (vv 31, 33) whom God had compensated by opening her womb: her sons will now avenge their and their mother's humiliation on the "hated" Joseph.

The fissure that threatens Jacob's family deepens with the dreams Joseph now dreams, and with his naive decision to recount them to his brothers. Many years previously, his father had wanted superiority over his brother, through birthright and blessing; now, Joseph dreams a pair of dreams that revolve around his ascendance over his siblings. We will not use these pages to analyze Joseph's dreams and the future implications they carry, since Jacob remains the focus of our attention. It is worth noting, however, that the son's appetite surpasses his father's: in the first dream, the sheaves of his brothers bow before Joseph's sheaf (v 7) and his brothers realize Joseph's powerful desire to rule over them (v 8); in the second, the sun, moon, and stars bow before him, showing us how Joseph stands above and beyond even the heavens (v 9). In this second dream, we see how the pupil has exceeded his teacher: Jacob, in his dream, had lain on the earth, stairway and angels above him, and God above all. Joseph's hubris, in contrast, knows no bounds. The brothers' reaction is natural, "and his brothers were jealous of him" (v 11), while the father's response is ambiguous. On one hand, Jacob tries to dismiss the dream as absurd—the image of the moon makes no sense, since Rachel has already died— perhaps in a desperate attempt to suppress the brothers' grow- ing indignation: "What is that dream that you have dreamed? Are we to come, I and your mother and your brothers, to bow down before you to the ground?" (v 10; the Rabbis explained: "'I and your mother,' yet your mother has already died, and you say I and your mother?" [*Genesis Rabbah* 64:11]). On the other hand, he understands the gravity of the dream's implica- tions: "and his father kept the matter in mind" (v 11). Dreams, Jacob knows, are not to be shrugged off.

After this seemingly considered response to Joseph's dreams, the reader may be baffled by Jacob's remarkable lack of caution in the very next scene. Jacob's sons are out with their father's flock in Shechem, far from home. Joseph has been left home— a strange state of affairs, seeing as Joseph, we had been told, "tend[s] the flock with his brothers . . ." (v 2). The author of the Testaments of the Twelve Patriarchs explained this incon- sistency: "Now, Joseph had been shepherding the flocks with us for about a month, and, delicate as he was, he was affected by the heat and taken ill. And he returned to Hebron to our father, and he made him lie down near him, because he loved him" (Testament of Gad 1:4–5).

Jacob knew of the older brothers' hatred and jealousy of Joseph. Nevertheless, he decides to send the youth on an er- rand: "Your brothers are pasturing at Shechem. Come, I will send you to them" (v 13). Even before Jacob defines the assign- ment more exactly—"Go and see how your brothers are and how the flock are and bring me back word" (v 14)—the young messenger hurries to accept the assignment, "Here I am," betraying his own failure to acknowledge his brothers' hostile feelings. But the father's foolishness borders on recklessness: had Jacob sent the boy to apprise him of the well-being of his other sons, we might be able to understand. But the fact that he asks to receive a report on the well-being of the flock, too, means that he sends Joseph to evaluate his brothers' competence as shepherds: Joseph is being sent to check up on his brothers! Not only was Jacob not troubled by Joseph's previous act of tattling, it turns out that he encouraged it! In sending Joseph as "overseer," Jacob plays with fire. When we consider his own experience of fraternal enmity and jealousy, it is truly baffling how he could have dispatched his beloved son to a similar fate, to brothers who hate him.

The bitter meeting between Joseph and his brothers concludes, of course, with Joseph's being thrown into a pit and sold off to Egypt. To their father the brothers will send the emblem of both his love and partiality, the ornamented tunic: "And they took Joseph's tunic and they slaughtered a he-goat, and dipped the tunic in its blood. And they sent the ornamented tunic and they brought it to their father, and they said, 'We found this. Identify it, please—Is it your son's tunic or not?'" (vv 31–32). Jacob believes the evidence: "And he identified it and said, 'It is my son's tunic. A savage beast has devoured him, Joseph was torn by a beast!'" (v 33).

There is an awkwardness in the verses I have just cited: the brothers, we are told, send the tunic and also bring it with them. Because of this, "and they sent it" (*vayeshalḥu*) has sometimes been read not as the verb *shalaḥ* ("to send") but as a denominal from *shelaḥ*, "sword," meaning something like "punctured, sliced [with a sword]." This was how the problem was solved in the Testament of Zebulun: "For they had stripped Joseph of our father's tunic when they were about to sell him and had put a slave's old coat on him. Now Simeon had the tunic and would not give it up, and he wanted *to cut it in pieces with his sword*, because he was angry Joseph was still alive and had not been killed" (4:10–11).

Whatever the case, his sons' cruel trickery represents one more measure-for-measure punishment for Jacob's having procured his brother's blessing: he cheated his father by using his brother's garments, now his own sons cheat him by using the garment of their brother. Moreover, we have already noted that Esau's fine clothes, his *bigdei hahamudot*, were really *bigdei hahamutsot*, sour-smelling clothes stained with the blood of the animals Esau hunted. With this meaning, the correspondence between the transgression and its punishment is tightened even further: Jacob tricked his father with foul-smelling, blood-stained garments, just as he is now deceived with a garment dipped in blood! The one who (falsely) played the role of hunter now believes (falsely) that his son has been hunted.

Jacob grieves for his son. Confronted with Joseph's garment, he tears his own: "And Jacob rent his clothes, put sackcloth on his loins and mourned for his son many days" (v 34). On sending Jacob to Haran, Jacob's mother had expected—wrongly— that their separation would last only "a few days" (27:44); Jacob, who wrongly assumes that his son has died, now grieves inconsolably for "many days"—one more example of the biblical writer's sense of literary justice. We, who know how Jacob has been fooled, respond otherwise, like Jacob who, after Joseph's dream, "kept the matter in mind" (v 11).

Joseph's brothers watch their father's torment, having no choice but to continue the masquerade—"All his sons and daughters sought to console him" (v 35)—though Jacob is not comforted: "but he refused to be consoled, saying, 'No, I will go down to my son mourning to Sheol.' And his father bewailed him."

Jacob's mourning indeed lasts "many days"—that is, many years. Joseph was seventeen when he was torn from his father's house, and he is thirty when we see him next, standing before Pharaoh with the solution to that ruler's dreams, telling of seven years of abundance and seven years of famine that will follow (Gen 41). The seven years of plenty pass before Jacob sends his sons to procure food in Egypt, though this does not lead to an immediate meeting between son and father. On the contrary, there are yet more trials for Jacob to face before he will learn that Joseph lives, and before they are reunited.

As the famine in Canaan persists, ten of Jacob's sons make their way to Egypt. Benjamin—Rachel's other son—has been left at home with Jacob, "for he said, 'lest disaster befall him'" (42:4). Perhaps, we think, Jacob has finally learned the danger of entrusting the elder sons with those of his beloved Rachel. When the brothers arrive in Egypt they meet Joseph, now the king's regent, who decides to test them. Hiding his identity (a strategy remarkably similar to the one adopted years ago by his father), Joseph accuses his brothers of espionage and forces them to return to Canaan without Simeon, the second oldest (Reuben he sends back with the others because—we now learn—he protected Joseph when the others wanted to kill him). Joseph wants the brothers to return with Benjamin—to test, he tells them, whether they are being truthful regarding their stated purpose for being in Egypt, that is, to find food for their family. Of course, Joseph's real objective is to determine whether the brothers had ever felt remorse for their actions, whether they had repented for having sold him, and whether they would now treat the young Benjamin, his only full brother, differently.

The brothers' test is a severe one for the father, too. Will Jacob allow Benjamin to return with his brothers to Egypt in order to free Simeon? At first he refuses: "It is me that you bereave: Joseph is no more, Simeon is no more, and you would take Benjamin! It is I who endures it all!" (42:36). Reuben's attempt to persuade his father to entrust Benjamin to their care, and his willingness to assume full responsibility should they fail—"my two sons you may kill if I do not bring him back to you . . ." (v 37)—meet with failure. Could the death of his two grandsons, his own blood, compensate for the loss of his son? Jacob is adamant: "My son shall not go down with you, for his brother is dead and he alone is left. Should disaster befall him on the road that you take him, you would send my whitened head in grief to Sheol" (v 38). Jacob's words resemble those he spoke when he first learned of Joseph's (supposed) fate: " . . . for I will go down to my son mourning to Sheol" (37:35).

But the famine intensifies and pushes Jacob to do the unthinkable. When the provisions brought from Egypt are depleted, Jacob is again forced to send his sons southward. This time he reluctantly also sends Benjamin, after Judah, standing now as the brothers' leader and speaking with more wisdom than had Reuben, tells him: "I will be his surety; you may hold me responsible: if I do not bring him to you and present him before you, I will be guilty before you for all time" (43:9). With no other options, Jacob places his trust in God: "take your brother, rise, and return to the man. And may El Shaddai grant you mercy before the man and release to you your other brother [Simeon], and Benjamin. As for me, if I must be bereaved, I shall be bereaved" (v 14). Jacob's dread at sending Benjamin with the brothers returns us, with great immediacy, to the day he lost Joseph after sending him to check on his brothers. Joseph, we assume, does not mean to torture his father, to add to the old man's sufferings, but the trial with which he now tests his brothers is, in fact, a secondary punishment—from God—for Jacob, both for his duplicity toward his own father as well as for his having favored one son above the others. Readers—and clearly also Jacob himself—experience a strong sense of déjà vu.

With the brothers' arrival in Egypt there awaits one last difficult test in which they will be forced to prove their resolve not to abandon Benjamin. Joseph, who emerges as a director of unparalleled talent, commands his house steward to place into Benjamin's bag a goblet—the goblet he uses for divination—at the moment that the brothers are set to leave. Once they have departed, Joseph dispatches men to pursue them and the goblet is found, of course, with Benjamin, who is promptly accused of theft.

Joseph doesn't realize that the trial he has so cleverly constructed represents the closing of an older account. In a variation of the measure-for-measure principle—an intergenerational version of which is referred to explicitly in Jeremiah 31:29 as "parents ate sour grapes and [their] children's teeth are blunted"—this punishment is, in fact, directed at Rachel, Joseph's mother, who (we recall) stole her father's terafim before she and Jacob fled him (a story that began in 31:19). Many correspondences can be found between the two episodes: Jacob set out with his family for Canaan, while Jacob's sons now set out from Egypt on their way to Canaan; the terafim stolen by Rachel were used for divination, as was the goblet "stolen" by Benjamin (this is stated explicitly in 44:5, 15). In both stories, a group of men pursue those who flee and overtake them (31:23, 25; 44:4, 6); Laban and Joseph both accuse the runaways with thievery (31:30; 44:4, see also v 15); the suspects, certain of their innocence, declare their and their household's righteousness and are ready to renounce the guilty one—if, indeed, he or she exists—to be punished with death (31:32; 44:9). A search takes place: the last stop in the search for Laban's terafim is Rachel's tent (31:34–35), and in the search for the goblet, the bag of the youngest brother (44:12). Finally, both stories conclude harmoniously (31:43–32:1; 45:1–15).

These many parallels, however, cannot obscure the inverse relationship of other resemblances: the mother who stole the terafim is not caught, whereas her son—who stole nothing— is. Jacob, whom Laban falsely accused of stealing the terafim and whose guilty wife was not caught, complains about Laban's suspicions (31:36–42); Joseph, the false accuser, is the one who complains about the theft (44:15). And, finally, Rachel, who is guilty, dies before Jacob and his household reach their destination (35:16–20), while her son Benjamin will not die for the transgression he did not commit.

The Rabbis, aware of the correspondence, added a scene after Benjamin is apprehended:

> They [the brothers] stand and hit Benjamin on his shoulders and say to him, "You are a thief, son of a thief. You have shamed us. You are the son of your mother—who likewise shamed our father," "and Rachel stole the terafim" (Gen 31:19). (*Tanḥuma Buber, Mikets* 13)

Joseph's brothers bear the trial valiantly. They refuse to abandon Benjamin and throw themselves onto the ground before Joseph (44:14), willing to share the burden of Benjamin's "guilt" and to become enslaved (v 16). Speaking at length, Judah begs to be able to fulfill the promise he made his father and become a slave to Joseph in Benjamin's stead (vv 18–34). These expressions of devotion to their brother and father do the trick. Judah's final words, "for how shall I go up to my father and the boy is not with me, lest I see the distress that will overtake my father" (v 34), bring Joseph to tears and push him to divulge his identity (45:1–3). Indeed, his love for his father overwhelms him and he blurts out: "I am Joseph. Is my father still alive?" (v 3). He tries to alleviate the brothers' consciences, "and now, it was not you that sent me here but God . . ." (v 8), and rushes to send them to their father: "Hurry and go up to my father and say to him, 'thus said your son Joseph, God has made me as a lord to all of Egypt. Come down to me, do not delay'" (v 9).

Joseph's brothers return to Canaan and their father, telling him the good news: "Joseph yet lives! And he is ruler over all the land of Egypt" (45:26). Jacob's first reaction of disbelief—

"And his heart went numb for he did not believe them"—is replaced by muted joy when he hears the message that Joseph has sent and when he sees the wagons Joseph sent him: "and the spirit of their father revived. And Israel said, 'Enough! Joseph my son lives! I shall go and see him before I die'" (45:28–46:1). Jacob, who had feared he would "go down to my son mourning to Sheol" (37:35), will now meet him in the land of the living.

On the way to Egypt Jacob stops in Beer-sheba, a place associated with his grandfather and father in two parallel stories. According to Genesis 21, Abraham sealed a pact with Abimelech, king of the Philistines, in Beer-sheba, the city having been named for the seven (*sheva‘*) ewes Abraham gave Abimelech as proof that he had dug the well (*be’er*) there (v 30) and also " . . . for there the two of them took an oath [*nishbe‘u*; the verb shares the same root as the word *sheva‘*]" (v 31). According to Genesis 26, however, Isaac's servants were the ones to dig the well (v 21), and Isaac was the one who sealed the eponymous pact with Abimelech in Beer-sheba: "they exchanged *oaths*" (v 31). Isaac was even granted a divine revelation in Beer-sheba (26:24), where he built an altar and invoked God's name (v 25), making Beer-sheba into a sacred place. This is the reason for Jacob's stopover and explains why he offers sacrifices there to "the God of his father Isaac" (46:1).

Like his father, Jacob is granted a nocturnal vision in the holy place—the single revelation of God in Joseph's lengthy biography—"And God spoke to Israel in a night-vision, and he said, 'Jacob, Jacob!' And he said, 'Here I am.' And He said, 'I am God, the God of your forefathers. Fear not to go down to Egypt for I will make you a great nation there" (46:2–3). Permission to descend to Egypt was necessary since God had forbidden Jacob's father from journeying there in similar circumstances of famine (26:1–2). But God grants Jacob permission because this descent has a particular purpose in God's plan for Jacob's family to become the nation to whom He will give the Land of Canaan. The last of God's words to Jacob in Beer-sheba are personal—"and Joseph will put out his hand to [close] your eyes" (v 4)—a promise that corresponds to Jacob's express desire to " . . . see him before I die" (45:28).

Jacob's wish is fulfilled. After such a dramatic buildup, having had to watch silently as Jacob was told the lie about Joseph's death, and after he—and we—have waited so long for this reunion, it is perhaps strange that the biblical authors did not give us a more detailed picture of the meeting. Instead, we are told only that Joseph went ahead to meet his father in Goshen and that, on meeting him, he embraced him "around the neck, he wept on his neck a good while" (46:29). This is, we remind ourselves, already Joseph's story, not Jacob's. Did Jacob tremble? Was he so overcome with emotion that his other sons had to hold his elbows to support him? We know only that he felt fulfilled and said, "Now I can die, after seeing your face, for you still live" (v 30). Only later will we realize that Jacob lives seventeen more years (47:28).

In his audience with Pharaoh, Jacob, a foreigner, blesses the king and, answering the Egyptian's question, reveals his age: "The days of the years of my sojourn [on earth] are one hundred and thirty years. Few and bad have been the days of the years of my life, and they did not reach the days of the years of my fathers in their sojourns" (47:9). One wonders why Jacob summarizes his life so negatively, particularly now, when he has lived to know that Joseph is alive and witness the fame and honor his son has achieved. Perhaps, with the dissipation of tension and excitement, Jacob feels the weight of his years. He looks back on his flight from Esau to Haran and recalls the years of servitude to Laban, the jealous rivalries between his wives, the death of Rachel just when they had returned to Canaan, the terrible events involving Dinah and Bilhah, and, particularly, the long years during which he had wished to die,

believing that his beloved Joseph had met his death in the claws
of a wild animal.

The report of Jacob's age on his arrival in Egypt enables
us to calculate the years the patriarchs lived in Canaan before
Jacob's descent to Egypt, according to the Book of Genesis:
Abraham was seventy-five when he arrived in Canaan (12:4);
twenty-five years later, at the age of one hundred, he fathered
Isaac (21:5). When Isaac was sixty he fathered Jacob (25:26),
and now Jacob is one hundred and thirty. The total number
of years that the patriarchs lived in Canaan before arriving in
Egypt, therefore, was two hundred and fifteen. When the time
comes for them to leave Egypt, we will learn the number of
years of their servitude there: "And the sojourn of the Israelites who sojourned in Egypt was thirty years and four hundred
years" (Exod 12:40). The Septuagint and the Samaritan Pentateuch preserve a different version: "And the sojourn of the
Israelites who sojourned *in the Land of Canaan and in the Land
of Egypt* was thirty years and four hundred years," meaning that
the number of years they were in Egypt was exactly the number of years they had been in Canaan. In our Masoretic text,
the principle is different: for every year that our forefathers
spent in Canaan, they spent two in Egypt. The intention of this
chronological information would seem to have been to signal
that, in Canaan, the patriarchs—and particularly Jacob—did
things that should not have been done, for which they were
sentenced to servitude in Egypt. The twofold proportion—two
years in Egypt for every one in Canaan—is also reflected in Isaiah 40:2: "Speak tenderly to Jerusalem, and declare to her that
her term of service is over, that her iniquity is expiated; for she
has received at the hand of the Lord *double* for all her sins."

We return to Jacob. While Jacob is alive, and while Pharaoh and Joseph live, the family fares well. Jacob and his household settle in the land of Goshen, where they are isolated from

the native Egyptian population—an expression of the isolationist ideology, according to which the patriarchs remained apart from the native populations in both Canaan and Egypt. For the biblical writers, the Israelites' isolationism was necessary to safeguard the young, monotheistic nation and to emphasize its uniqueness. Joseph supports the family during the years of famine (47:12) and they become a nation: "Thus Israel settled in the land of Egypt, in the land of Goshen, and they acquired holdings in it and they were fruitful and they increased greatly" (v 27).

Seventeen years pass and Jacob senses his approaching death. The many years he has lived in Egypt, his second exile, have not caused him to forget the land that was promised him and his descendants, and he makes Joseph take an oath to bring him to burial in the grave of his ancestors (vv 29–31). Abraham was born outside Canaan and died in Canaan; Isaac was born and died in Canaan (having never left); Jacob was born in Canaan but dies abroad. Jacob wants all three generations to find eternal rest together, in one place.

Another meeting between Joseph and Jacob before the father's death (or, in another version, soon after the meeting described in 47:29–31) is described in chapter 48. Joseph appears here with the two sons he has fathered in Egypt, Manasseh and Ephraim (v 1). First, Jacob reminds Joseph of the blessing he received from God in Luz, in the Land of Canaan: "And he said to me, 'I will make you fertile and numerous, making of you a community of peoples; and I will assign this land to your offspring to come for an everlasting possession'" (v 4). And truly, in Jacob's words we hear echoes of the blessing that God had given him following his return from Paddan-Aram (35:11–12). That same blessing that he received then, of fruitfulness and of being given the Promised Land, Jacob now tries to pass on to the sons of his beloved Joseph: "And now, your two sons who were born to you in the land of Egypt before my coming to you in Egypt, shall be mine; Ephraim and Manasseh shall be to me like Reuben and like Simeon" (v 5). Readers might assume that Jacob has learned his lesson: his father had wanted to bless only Esau, while here we find Jacob apparently wanting to bless both Joseph's sons with one, binding blessing. But a careful reading of the verses reveals that the two sons are not equal in Jacob's estimation, since he places the younger before the older, "Ephraim and Manasseh." A few moments later it becomes obvious that Jacob indeed wants to preserve the model that he helped establish: the priority of the younger son over the firstborn.

Jacob's next words seem to digress from the matter at hand. He suddenly mentions Rachel's death: "and I, when I was coming from Paddan, Rachel died to my sorrow in the land of Canaan on the way, still some distance from Ephrath, and I buried her there on the way to Ephrath—that is Bethlehem" (v 7). But the digression makes sense: in this, his last, intimate meeting with Rachel's son, Jacob wants to share with him the terrible event that occurred immediately following—and in complete variance to—the blessing he had received in Luz (note the juxtaposition of 35:9–15 with 35:16–20). Only Joseph can share his father's sense of loss and grief, which has remained strong after all this time. For years Jacob thought that Joseph had died, believed that he would go to Joseph "mourning to Sheol" (37:35); now he knows he will leave Joseph in the land of the living and descend to Sheol to meet Rachel, the love of his life.

As Jacob mentions Ephraim and Manasseh, he is unaware that they are standing beside his bed, because his eyes "were heavy with age; he could not see" (v 10). The storyteller refers to his blindness only when Jacob turns to bless Joseph's sons directly, without intermediaries, once again creating a strong sense of déjà vu in the reader's mind—"And Isaac was old and his eyes were too dim to see" (27:1). We remember the consequences of Isaac's blindness when he blessed his sons, and we are therefore curious to know the implications of Jacob's on the blessing of his two sonlike grandsons.

When Jacob announces his intent to bless Ephraim and Manasseh, Joseph—aware of his father's weak vision—takes care to position them so that the firstborn will receive the preferred blessing: "And Joseph took the two of them, Ephraim with his right hand to Israel's left and Manasseh with his left hand to Israel's right and presented them to him" (v 13). But Jacob does the unexpected: "And Israel extended his right hand and laid it on the head of Ephraim, though he is the younger, and his left hand on the head of Manasseh, crossing his hands, for Manasseh was the firstborn" (v 14). Before Joseph can recover from his surprise, Jacob has already begun a joint blessing over the two:

> The God before whom walked my fathers Abraham and Isaac, the God who has shepherded me all my life to this very day, the angel who has redeemed me from all evil—may he bless these lads. In them may my name be recalled, and the names of my fathers Abraham and Isaac, and may they teem multitudes upon the earth. (vv 15–16)

By all appearances, Jacob seems to bless his two grandsons with a single blessing, thus preventing jealousies and conflict. But Joseph is not fooled: with Jacob's right hand placed on Ephraim's head, he understands that the younger brother is likely to receive the stronger part of the blessing, and his suspicion is swiftly confirmed: the word Jacob uses to bless the boys and their descendants with fertility and growth, *veyidgu*, is from the root *d-g-h*, a synonym of *p-r-h* ("to be fruitful"), the root we hear in the name Ephraim, and therefore covertly interprets that name and alludes to the fact that Ephraim is the blessing's primary beneficiary. Joseph hurries to intervene, and before he even speaks he moves to correct his father: "And Joseph saw that his father was placing his right hand on Ephraim's head and it was wrong in his eyes and he took hold of his father's hand to move it from Ephraim's head to the head of Manasseh. And Joseph said to his father, 'Not so, Father. For this is the first-born. Place your right hand on his head'" (vv 17–18). Joseph, who has perhaps suffered the most from sibling jealousy, wants to prevent the troubled sibling relations that have plagued generations of his father's family from characterizing his own sons' relations. Jacob, however, insists. The old patriarch seems to know what lies ahead. His blindness has not engendered confusion: what he has done has been deliberate. "But his father objected, saying, 'I know, my son, I know. He, too, shall be a people and he, too, shall be great. Yet his younger brother shall be greater than he, and his seed shall be plentiful enough for nations" (v 19)—confirmation that Ephraim's abundant fruitfulness was indeed alluded to previously. Jacob speaks as one who has been given the prophetic spirit, as one whose spiritual vision now compensates for physical blindness and allows him to see farther, to gaze into the future to the time when the tribe of Ephraim will dominate, whether during the conquest of the Land of Canaan by Joshua, son of Nun, an Ephraimite, or during the founding of the Kingdom of Israel, the northern kingdom, under the reign of the Ephraimite Jeroboam.

Joseph's interruption causes Jacob to again bless the two boys, once more with a single blessing that reaffirms Ephraim's precedence over Manasseh: "By you [singular; in the Septuagint it is the plural] shall Israel bless, saying, 'May God set you as Ephraim and Manasseh'" (v 20). To remove any remaining doubt, the storyteller adds explicitly: "And he placed Ephraim before Manasseh."

I have said that Jacob spoke with the spirit of prophecy; this is to say, it was not capriciousness but foreknowledge that caused him to place his right hand on Ephraim. Jacob was not trying to direct the future with his blessing, but to open a window through which the future might be glimpsed. Nonetheless,

it's impossible not to sense a personal motive in his preference: at the end of his life, in this moment of personal account-
taking and summing up, it was important for Jacob to under-
score God's desire for blessing the younger sons. God was the
one who desired his precedence over Esau, God viewed with
favor his preferential love for Joseph, and God was the one who
chose Ephraim over Manasseh. With the blessing of Ephraim
and Manasseh, therefore, we have a sort of act of repair, a *tikun*,
of Jacob's stealing the blessing from Esau, and his blessing over
his two grandsons instills a calm contentment in Jacob at this
late moment just before his death.

10

---

*"Gather together that I may tell you what is to
befall you in the days to come":
An End, A Beginning*

IN CONTRAST to his father and grandfather, who each left
one heir destined to continue the family line and make mani-
fest the divine promise, Jacob leaves twelve sons, evidence that
God's promise has already begun to be fulfilled and that Jacob-
Israel will indeed become the founder of a nation. Jacob knows
this—through a prophetic spirit—and he gathers his sons in
order to inform them about "what is to befall you in the days
to come" (Gen 49:1). Jacob's words reveal a change in his character: he has become a prophet. Indeed, with this chapter we
witness the transformation of Jacob, the man who fathered
many sons, into Israel, the father of the nation. Jacob addresses
his sons one by one, but his words are really directed at their
descendants: "All these are the tribes of Israel, twelve, and this
is what their father spoke to them and blessed them, each one
according to his blessing he blessed them" (v 28).

"The Blessing of Jacob" reminds us of Moses' prophetic

blessing of the tribes on the eve of his death in Deuteronomy 33. These two appended collections of prophecies divide the Pentateuch in two: the Book of Genesis, ending with Jacob's blessing, tells the story of a family, the nation's founders; the first chapter of Exodus on, until the blessing of Moses at the end of Deuteronomy, tells the history of the nation and their transition from slavery to redemption. The next books of the Bible tell of the Israelites' life in their own land. The two "blessings" therefore denote transitions and foretell what awaits: from family to nation, and from nomadic to settled life in the Promised Land.

As a whole, Jacob's blessing/prophecy is a mosaic of discrete elements, some quite archaic and difficult (if not impossible) to understand. It is a collection of sayings representing different literary genres from dissimilar origins, illuminating the nature of the different tribes. Several of the sons/tribes are likened to animals (tribal totems, perhaps?); several of the sayings supply interpretations of the son's/tribe's name, which reveal the tribe's destiny; some allude to the primary livelihood of the tribe; some to the geographic territory where they reside.

The preamble signals the shift from the sons of Jacob to the tribes of Israel: "Gather and listen, Jacob's sons, listen to Israel your father" (v 2). The order of the blessings diverges from the sons' birth order, so that all of Leah's sons come first (vv 3–15), and Rachel's two sons come last (vv 22–23). In between come Bilhah's and Zilpah's sons, in a chiastic order: Bilhah's son Dan (vv 16–18), followed by both of Zilpah's sons, Gad and Asher (vv 19–20), followed by Bilhah's younger son, Naphtali (v 21).

The so-called blessings of Leah's first four sons comprise a unit unto themselves, constructed according to the three-four pattern—the same pattern followed in the story of their births. Here, Jacob not only condemns but curses his three eldest sons, Reuben, Simeon, and Levi, making clear the reasons for their having been denied firstborn rights. In contrast, he blesses his fourth son, Judah, to whom is given power and rule over his brothers.

Reuben is condemned: "Unstable as water, you shall excel no longer ['al totar, i.e., you will lose the birthright], for when you mounted your father's bed, you defiled my couch, you mounted!" (v 4). Another possible meaning of 'al totar is "you shall not increase," that is, "you shall not reproduce" (cf. Moses' blessing of the tribe of Reuben: "May Reuben live and not die, though few be his numbers" [Deut 33:6]).

I have already written how the story of Reuben and Bilhah in Genesis 35:21–22 was meant to explain this perplexing curse, and how the story precedes it in order to forestall our wonder. I also mentioned how the story there ended abruptly after the words "and Israel heard" (v 22), in order to imply that the response would ultimately arrive, as it now does.

Jacob next addresses Simeon and Levi. He is so enraged at the two that he avoids addressing them directly and speaks in the third person: "Simeon and Levi, brothers, their weapons are tools of lawlessness" (v 5). Jacob seeks to distance himself from them: "In their council let my person not be included, in their assembly let my presence not be counted. For when enraged they slaughtered men, at their pleasure they maimed oxen" (v 6).

We might be able to understand violence committed in a fit of fury (even if we do not approve), but these brothers also committed violence for the sake of pleasure—"at their pleasure they maimed oxen"—behavior that cannot be tolerated. For this reason Jacob curses the two sons/tribes: "Cursed be their rage so fierce, their wrath so ferocious! I will divide them in Jacob, scatter them in Israel" (v 7). The curse provides an explanation for the historical disappearance of the tribe of Simeon when it became absorbed into the tribe of Judah (see Josh 19:1; 1 Chron 4:24–43), and for the fact that the tribe of Levi—unlike the others—had no territory of its own. We have already stated (chapter 7) that the incorporation of the verses about Simeon and Levi into the Dinah story in Genesis 34 was an interpretation, a preemptive midrash, so to speak, of the curse they now receive from their father in Genesis 49:5–7, an attempt to provide a concrete example of the violent natures to which it refers and thus to justify their punishment.

The antithesis of the curses of the three older sons can be found in the blessing of Judah: "Judah, you [in contrast to your three older brothers] your brothers shall praise, your hand on your enemies' nape, and your father's sons shall bow down to you" (v 8).

Specific references to Judah's dominion are made later in this lengthy blessing of the tribe of Judah, which is, itself, like a mosaic: "The scepter shall not pass from Judah, nor the ruling stick from between his legs [a symbol of dominion] until he comes to Shiloh and the homage of peoples be his" (v 10). Behind the words "until he comes to Shiloh" may hide an intertribal conflict. Shiloh was an important cultic city in Ephraim and the site of the temple of Eli and Samuel (1 Sam 1–4); it was the city in which God initially dwelled prior to choosing Jerusalem (see Jer 7:12; Ps 78:60 ff.). Its presence here, in this expression of the power and dominion of the tribe of Judah, is therefore puzzling. It is possible that in the original version of the verse was written not *shiloh* but *shalem*, "until he comes to Shalem," one of the names for Jerusalem (see Gen 18:18; Ps 76:3)—an allusion to the rise of the House of David and to David's choice of Jerusalem as his capital city. A later writer's desire to assert the superiority of Ephraim over Judah—something we will see again, in the blessing of Joseph—caused the change from *sh-l-m* to *sh-l-h*, a switch of only one letter.

Next is Zebulun: "Zebulun on the shore of the seas shall dwell; he shall be the shore for ships, his flank shall rest on

Sidon" (v 13). Zebulun's name is covertly interpreted (using *sh-k-n*, "dwell," a synonym of *z-b-l*). The blessing demonstrates our scant knowledge of the geographic history of the biblical period. According to the Book of Joshua, the territory of Asher separated Zebulun's territory from the sea (9:10–16), though Deuteronomy's blessing of Moses supports our text. Zebulun and Issachar both benefited, according to Moses' blessing, from the livelihood they drew from the sea: " . . . for the seas' abundance they suckle and the hidden hoards of the sand" (Deut 33:19).

The blessing of Issachar includes both a comparison to an animal as well as a covert name etymology: "Issachar is a strong-boned donkey, crouching among the sheepfolds. When he saw how good was security, and how pleasant was the country, he bent his shoulder to the burden and became a toiling serf" (49:14–15). Issachar is likened to a donkey, ready and able for hard labor. Penned in by the sheepfold, he doesn't ask for his own freedom so long as he can work the fecund land of his territory in the lower Galilee. An etymology hides in verse 15: "and he bent his shoulder to the burden and became a toiling *serf* ['*oved*]": he puts his neck to the load, to *servitude*, from the root *'-b-d* which is synonymous with *s-kh-r*, the root heard in Issachar's name.

Following Leah's six sons, Jacob proceeds to those of the concubines, the first being Dan, Bilhah's firstborn. The blessing contains two unrelated elements, a name etymology and a likeness to an animal: "Dan shall judge [*yadin*] his people, as one of the tribes of Israel" (v 16). One of the smallest of the tribes (in Gen 46:23 Dan is said to have fathered only one son; this was probably one of the reasons for his portrayal as the son of a concubine), Jacob blesses Dan that he will judge, that he will be able to lead an independent tribe "as one of the tribes of Israel," tribes that were larger and stronger. In this verse we find the first appearance in the Bible of the term *shivtei yisra'el*, "tribes of Israel," which presumes the existence of a nation comprising a collection of tribes.

The second part of Dan's blessing likens him to a snake: "Dan shall be a snake on the road, a viper on the path that bites the horse's heels and its rider topples backwards" (49:17). The metaphor describes Dan as a tribe that uses guerrilla warfare, perhaps even as highway bandits who operate on the roadways, robbers who attack caravans as they pass on the trade routes bordering their territory, whether in the south "in the camp of Dan between Tsora and Eshta'ol" (Judg 13:25) or in the northern territory to which the tribe migrated, in the upper Galilee (Josh 19:47; Judg 18:27–29).

From Bilhah's firstborn, Jacob moves to Gad, whose territory is on the eastern side of the Jordan: "Gad shall be raided by raiders, but he shall raid at their heel [*gad gedud yegudenu vehu' yagud 'aqev*—a wonderfully alliterative covert name etymology]" (v 19). The short depiction that covertly interprets Gad's name fits nicely abutting Jacob's blessing of Dan, since here the picture is of guerrilla fighters who attack the enemy's backside, on his heel. In the annals of history Gad earned the reputation of a belligerent tribe, such as in Moses' blessing, in which the tribe is likened to a lion: "Blessed is the one who enlarges Gad! Like a lion he dwells and tears the arm and even scalp" (Deut 33:20). Next is Asher, whose fertile territory sits in the western Galilee: "Asher's bread shall be rich [lit., "fat," *shmenah*], and he shall yield kingly delicacies" (v 20). Then comes Bilhah's younger son Naphtali, who is likened to a doe, a quick and sure-footed animal who climbs with ease over the rocky mountains of the upper Galilee, the territory of the tribe of Naphtali.

The final sons to receive their blessings are those of Jacob's beloved Rachel, first Joseph and then Benjamin. The blessing to Joseph stretches out over four verses (as did Judah's), a testament to his importance. It is full of riddles, beginning with a comparison of Joseph to a wild ass (v 22) and telling also of his battles, of the enemies who attacked him—"They assailed him, they shot at him and harried him, the archers" (v 23)— whom he answers with war: "But his bow remained taut and his arms were ever-moving" (v 24). The rest of the verse, however, reveals that Joseph's source of strength was God: "By the hands of the Mighty One of Jacob, from there, the Shepherd, the Rock of Israel." The reading is difficult: it seems that one letter has been omitted from the word we have translated as "from there," *misham* (probably because of the *resh* at the beginning of the next word, *ro'eh*, "shepherd"); it should be read not *misham* but *mishomer*, "from the *shepherd*, from the *keeper*." Jacob has already described God as his shepherd, when he told Joseph, "God who has shepherded me all my life to this very day" (Gen 48:15). Jacob calls God a shepherd, also the Rock of Israel, *'even yisra'el*, an exact equivalent to the more common *tsur yisra'el* (e.g., 2 Sam 23:3). But perhaps the word *'even* was used here because of its previous significance in Jacob's story, so that it is an allusion to Jacob's God, the God of Bethel (see chapter 3), and the verse should be read: "By the hands of the Mighty One of Jacob, the Keeper, the Shepherd, the Rock of Israel."

The blessing's conclusion, "May they rest on the head of Joseph, on the brow of the elect of his brothers" (v 26b), places Joseph as the foremost brother: he is the "elect" (*nazir*) of his brothers, the wearer of the *nezer*, the crown. Giving dominion to Joseph creates a problem, however, since the power to rule has already been given to Judah (vv 8–10). A comparison between the second part of Joseph's blessing (vv 25b–26) with Moses' blessing to Joseph in Deuteronomy 33:13–16 helps to resolve the difficulty.

Moses' blessings set only one son at the top: Joseph. From the comparison of the passages we realize that verses 25–26 in

Genesis 49 were added under the influence of Moses' blessing, in order to cloud Judah's status and promote Joseph's. The insertion of Jacob's blessing into the Joseph cycle (Gen 37–48; 50), which naturally portrays Joseph as the foremost brother, triggered the emendation in the father's blessing, and Judah and his kingdom became pushed into the shadow cast by the Kingdom of Ephraim, the Kingdom of Israel (i.e., Joseph's descendants).

The last of the sons to be blessed is the youngest, Benjamin: "Benjamin is a ravenous wolf. In the morning he consumes the booty, in the evening divides the spoil" (v 27). Benjaminite territory lay between the mountainous regions of Judah and Ephraim and included the area's primary north-south road. The Benjaminites (according to Jacob's blessing) were highway robbers who plundered the caravans that passed through their territory. The wolf, the dusk-to-dawn hunter of shepherds who shares its kill with the pack, was chosen to represent the tribe. It is a surprising comparison, different from the submissive image of Benjamin that emerges from the Joseph story where he is the son of Jacob's old age, cared for by his brothers who fears for his well-being.

Now that he has foretold his sons' futures, the futures that await the twelve tribes, Jacob is ready to close his eyes. Still, he must complete one more task and ensure his burial in the grave of his forefathers in Canaan. Already before blessing Joseph and his sons, Jacob had foreseen his approaching death and had made Joseph swear that he would not be buried in Egypt but be brought to burial in his ancestral grave (47:29–31). Now, with the conclusion of the blessings to all his sons, Jacob commands them regarding his burial and the exact location of the grave:

> . . . bury me with my forefathers in the cave that is in the field
> of Ephron the Hittite. In the cave that is in the Machpelah
> field, which faces Mamre, in the Land of Canaan, the field

that Abraham bought from Ephron the Hittite for a burial site. There they buried Abraham and Sarah his wife, there they buried Isaac and Rebekah his wife; and there I buried Leah—the field and the cave in it, bought from the Hittites. (vv 29–32)

Jacob's words return us to the story of Abraham's purchase of land near Hebron for Sarah's burial (Gen 23), to the verses telling of his own burial there (25:9–10), and also the burial of his son Isaac (25:27–29). Now we learn, too, that Rebekah and Leah were buried in the same cave. Jacob's repeated instructions that he be buried in Canaan in the ancestral burial site is meant to emphasize the notion that Israel's settlement in Egypt was but a sojourn that did not signal abandonment of the wish to return to Canaan. God had revealed himself to Jacob when Jacob was on his way to Egypt, in Beer-sheba, and had promised him that "I myself will go down with you to Egypt and I myself will also bring you back up . . ." (46:4). The return of Jacob's body to Canaan for burial will therefore signify the first stage in the fulfillment of that divine promise, a sign of what is to come, of the return of the nation to its land and birthplace.

Jacob, the family's patriarch who has foreseen their transformation into a people and nation, is finally able to die in peace: "And Jacob finished charging his sons and he drew his feet up to the bed and breathed his last and he was gathered to his people" (v 33).

Jacob dies, but the story of his life does not reach its conclusion until the fulfillment of his last command, when his body will be brought for burial to Canaan. It is to the mourning Joseph that the spotlight now turns: "And Joseph flung himself upon his father's face and wept over him and kissed him" (50:1). Following Egyptian practice, Joseph commands his father's body be embalmed, a process that takes forty days, and all Egypt observes a mourning period of seventy days (vv 2–3).

Despite his position and authority, Joseph cannot leave Egypt without the permission of his lord. He conveys his request to the king: "My father made me swear, saying, 'I am about to die. In the grave that I dug [*kariti*] for myself in the land of Canaan, there you will bury me. And now, let me go up, and I will bury my father and I will return'" (v 5). Joseph's words awaken our astonishment: whether we understand the root *k-r-h* according to its usual meaning of "dig" (as in Ps 7:16) or we understand it as "purchase" (as in Hos 3:2), the verse cannot refer to Jacob's burial in the cave of Machpelah! Jacob did not *dig* a grave for himself in the cave of Machpelah, and he certainly did not purchase it with money, since it had already been bought by his grandfather. It seems apparent, therefore, that our verse preserves a vestige of another tradition about the location of Jacob's burial. In chapter 7, we dealt with a story parallel to that of Abraham's purchase of the cave of Machpelah, a tradition that told of Jacob's purchase of a piece of land in Shechem (Gen 33:18–20). Joseph will eventually be brought there for burial (see Josh 24:32: "The bones of Joseph, which the Israelites had brought up from Egypt, were buried in Shechem, in the piece of ground which Jacob had bought for a hundred kesitahs from the children of Hamor . . ."). When Joseph relates his father's words to Pharaoh in Genesis 50:5, he seems to refer to plans to bury Jacob in Shechem, in the piece of land that Jacob had purchased there, in which the bones of Joseph will also ultimately find their resting place.

The tradition that Jacob was buried in Shechem is found in the New Testament, in the overview of Israel's history as told by Stephen to the High Priest: "and Jacob went down into Egypt. And he died, himself and our fathers, and they were carried back to Shechem and laid in the tomb that Abraham had bought for a sum of silver from the sons of Hamor [son of] Shechem" (Acts 7:15–16). Though this tradition confuses a few things, identifying Abraham (not Jacob) as the one who purchased the parcel of land in Shechem, we must not dismiss lightly what it relates about the burial of Jacob in Shechem. Jacob's burial there perfectly concludes the depiction of this patriarch whose main activities are identified with the Kingdom of Israel (in Shechem, Bethel, Penuel). Like Abraham, who wandered through the territory that would later become the Kingdom of Judah, and purchased a tomb in Hebron where he would eventually be buried, so Jacob wanders in the future Kingdom of Israel and purchases his tomb in Shechem, a prominent city in the Kingdom of Israel, and it is there—according to one tradition—that he is buried.

Just as political considerations created varying traditions about Rachel's burial in Bethlehem (in Judah) and in Bethel (in Benjamin), divergent traditions regarding the location of Jacob's burial attest to political wrangling. The northern kingdom wanted Jacob for itself and claimed that he was buried in Shechem, in the piece of land he purchased in that cultic city, the first capital of the kingdom in the time of Jeroboam ben Nabat (1 Kings 12:25). The kingdom of Judah also claimed ownership of the patriarch's grave, and so formed the tradition of Jacob's having been buried with the rest of the nation's patriarchs in Hebron, David's first capital when he ruled over the tribe of Judah (1 Kings 2:11).

These traditions are evidence of how burials served political purposes. We are hardly surprised, therefore, when we learn how some individuals received more than one grave as more than one group claimed the deceased as their own, bequeathing contradictory traditions that cannot be brought into agreement. In the end, the Judahite tradition about Jacob's burial won out over the Israelite tradition, and the tale of Jacob's burial reaches its end in Hebron's cave of Machpelah (v 13). (Incidentally, according to the Testament of Joseph [20:6], all Jacob's sons were buried in the cave of Machpelah, as befits the nation's patriarchs.) These chapters about the end of

Jacob's life preserve conspicuous evidence of the Judah-Israel rivalry. Though the Judahite tradition prevailed in the matter of Jacob's burial, however, the textual change that we already noted, from "Shalem" to "Shiloh," and the addition of the verses about "elect of his brothers" to the blessing of Joseph reflect smaller victories for the writers from the north, from the Kingdom of Israel.

All of Egypt participates in the funerary procession:

> So Joseph went up to bury his father, and with him went up all the officials of the Pharaoh, the senior members of his court, and all of Egypt's dignitaries, together with all of Joseph's household, his brothers, and his father's household; only their children, their flocks, and their herds were left in the region of Goshen. Chariots, too, and horsemen went up with him; it was a very large troop. (vv 7–9)

To Egypt's seventy days of mourning are now added seven more days of lament "in Goren ha-Atad, which is on the other side of the Jordan." It seems that the Egyptians end their role there, in Goren ha-Atad. The more intimate procession then continues to Hebron as Jacob's family carries him to his final resting place. Jacob's sons return to Egypt following their father's funeral.

Jacob did not return home alive, but with his prophetic vision he saw the return of his sons—the twelve tribes of Israel—to the Land. Four books, and many centuries, will pass before we get to that stage in the nation's life, but Jacob-Israel, the patriarch who represents the transformation from family to nation, has sketched the outlines of that picture for us.

Conclusion

THE CONUNDRUM of this book is that it is a biography that
rests on a biography—on a relatively short life story (with em-
phasis on "story") that resembles (as biblical stories do, generally) a theater production in which the inner worlds of the
Bible's heroes are hidden from us, as is that of the narrator(s),
whose opinions are almost never expressed overtly. As we now
attempt to summarize what we have examined in the ten chapters of this book, we will do well to distinguish between our
conclusions concerning the mosaic that is the whole story of
Jacob's life, and those about the figure that peers back at us
from its carefully arranged collection of tales.

In the larger work we discerned parallel forces at play: on
one hand, the aim to describe Jacob's transgressions and the di-
vinely ordained penalties he suffered as a consequence; on the
other, attempts to assuage, to find extenuating circumstances,
and to improve Jacob's image. For his controversial transaction,

the purchase of the birthright from Esau, Jacob suffers by becoming, himself, merchandise traded in exchange for mandrakes between two sisters, Leah and Rachel. For deceiving his father and stealing the blessing intended for his brother, Jacob is punished again and again: he is exiled from his land (never to see his mother again); the woman he adores is replaced by her sister in his wedding bed (in a measure-for-measure scene of sibling substitution, darkness, and deceit)—ultimately resulting in Jacob's marrying two wives and their two maidservants, a fierce and bitter competition among the women for their husband's love, and subsequent jealousies between their sons. Tense relations between Jacob's sons propel events to the climactic selling of Joseph, along with Reuben's violation of Bilhah. Jacob is also punished with years of servitude under Laban, who changes his wages ten times. Worst of all, his sons, having learned deceit from their father, bring catastrophe when they lie to the Shechemites and to Jacob and, in the ultimate payback, hold up a blood-dipped garment (again according to the measure-for-measure principle) in order to persuade him how "Joseph was torn by a beast!" Joseph, too, increases his father's punishment when he bides his time before revealing his identity, demanding that Benjamin appear before him and thus reopening the older man's wound, the loss of Joseph.

Despite the narrative's precise account-keeping, with its assiduous insistence that the transgressor pay in full for his deeds, the mosaic's creators refrained from presenting an unambiguous picture. Instead, efforts were made to show us that our villain was not really so terrible. The most heroic expression of this tendency was the replacement of the original birth story of Jacob's in utero seizure of the birthright (a story that was widespread in the ancient oral tradition, and which we reconstructed), an act that earned him the name *ya'aqov* for having cheated his brother already at birth, with the more tempered, official story, according to which he was named for having grabbed his brother's heel, delaying the birthright's transfer until the twins were older. Esau is portrayed as willing to forgo the birthright—he even spurns it—proof that he was never worthy of it.

I have mentioned the stage of oral transmission that preceded the stories' being written and incorporated into the sacred corpus. Oral tales about the cool-headed and cunningly successful trickster were evidently quite popular among listeners in that stage, but their inclusion within the Israelites' sacred texts required a refinement and reevaluation of traditions. At the same time, the Bible's writers were prevented from obscuring entirely the essential lines of the original tales, lest their versions not appear credible and be rejected by readers who recognized and knew the stories' initial, oral versions.

Defensive forces were also mobilized to Jacob's aid regarding the accusation that he stole the blessing: the aged father's desire to bless Esau derived only from the fact that he enjoyed the savory game Esau supplied him; it was not Jacob but his mother who initiated the scheme for stealing the blessing and she, in any case, only sought to realize the oracle, "older younger shall serve," while he was compelled to follow her commands. A frame story was enlisted, too, in support of the defense, and is like the chocolate used to coat a bitter pill: Esau took foreign, Canaanite women as wives, proving his unworthiness to participate in the patriarchal relay race, to be entrusted with the responsibility of passing the baton onward. Finally, at the very end of the story, it becomes apparent that Isaac had kept the supreme blessing, the "blessing of Abraham," for Jacob after all, so that Jacob's departure for Haran was not a hurried escape from his brother's wrath but a journey made in order to find a suitable wife with whom he might father sons: proper descendants of the House of Abraham and Isaac.

Exoneration for Jacob's act of deception flickered, too, at the end of his life when, in granting his deathbed blessing to Joseph's sons, Manasseh and Ephraim, he retroactively legitimized his own blessing by giving priority to the younger Ephraim, knowing that this represented God's will.

Like Rebekah, who became burdened with part of her son's guilt in order to improve his image, so, too, was Rachel assigned blame for stealing her father's terafim—while Jacob only "stole" Laban's heart. For his "thievery," Jacob was entirely vindicated (God had wanted him to be free of Laban's clutches) whereas Rachel's clear-cut thievery caused her death (indirectly) and also incurred the punishment of her son Benjamin (according to the measure-for-measure principle) for a transgression that he did not commit, when the goblet Joseph used for predictions was found in his bag.

The story of Jacob's shrewd dealings with Laban's dishonest handling of his wages (the speckled and dark-colored sheep), when Jacob used magic and did not turn to God, also receives a "makeover" with the help of a flashback, when Jacob recounted to his wives how an angel had spoken to him in a dream and told him that God would not allow Laban to exploit him.

One more effort to cleanse Jacob comes from outside the Book of Genesis, when the new name given to Jacob, Israel, is explained as deriving from *yashar*, "honest, straight," that is, the opposite of the first meaning of *ya'aqov*. In this same spirit was the nation given the name Yeshurun.

We have observed the two conflicting forces at work in the formulation of Jacob's biography. It's time now to see if we can step back and, considering the mosaic in its entirety, distinguish the broad contours of Jacob's character. We see that Jacob alternately exhibited initiative and passiveness. He initiated (wrongly) the purchase of the birthright; successfully managed Laban's attempt to deny him his wages (revealing a bit of the trickster image that had been prevalent in the oral tradition); fled Laban in order to return home; and when he found himself at the gateway to Canaan, prepared meticulously for his meeting with his brother, even sending messengers to Esau with placating gifts.

In other scenes, Jacob does not lead but is led, sometimes even fleeing from responsibility. His mother was the one who initiated the stealing of the blessing and he obeyed; when Rachel, desperate, asked for his help, "give me sons" (30:1), he did not pray to God (in contrast to his father, who petitioned God on behalf of his wife, Rebekah); and when she attempted to solve the problem of her barrenness by using the mandrakes, he accepted the transaction sealed between her and her sister and wordlessly submitted to Leah's directive to "sleep with me, for I have hired you with my son's mandrakes" (v 16).

Jacob failed as a father, too. When told of Dinah's rape, he waited until his sons returned home, essentially giving them free rein to deceive the Shechemites and take revenge for their dishonored sister. And, having inherited his parents' habit of preferential love, Jacob favored his youngest son. He indulged Joseph and, though the other sons were jealous, neglected to take adequate action to avert approaching disaster. On the contrary, he sent Joseph to check on his other sons while they were shepherding his flocks, seemingly unaware of the awaiting danger. Jacob's preference for Joseph derived from his love for Rachel, a love for which he had been willing to pay with his freedom. Rachel's premature death at the end of the journey from Haran to the Land of Canaan left a permanent shadow on Jacob's heart, an experience he related much later to Joseph.

But the story of Jacob's life was not put into writing simply to recount what occurred. Historians have six eyes: two looking into the past, two for observing the present, and two for gazing into the future. The life stories that the Bible preserves were written to educate the writers' contemporaries, their children, and their children's children for generations. Let's look now at the covert messages, the hidden agenda bequeathed us by virtue of Jacob's life story.

As we have seen in this volume, the Bible's stories often championed political—territorial—convictions. We have focused solely on Jacob, isolating him from the course of the nation's history, but we mustn't forget that Jacob was only one link in the chain of generations, one stop in Israel's unfolding history. Jacob was the third of the nation's patriarchs, the grandson of Abraham and son of Isaac. In the introduction we asked whether this dynastic structure was artificial. Evidence seems to indicate this to be so. Abraham's life is set primarily in the region that would later become the territory of Judah—Hebron and Beer-sheba—while his reputation is even linked (if only secondarily and artificially) with Jerusalem. On his arrival in Canaan and on his way to the Negev (12:9), Abraham passed through the northern cities of Shechem and Bethel and built altars in both (vv 6–8), but these were only slight impressions resulting from assimilation to the traditions about his grandson Jacob, the reasons for which will be discussed momentarily.

Isaac—an intermediary, undeveloped figure in Genesis—was, like his father, a "southerner," but Jacob's activities revolved around cities later identified with the northern kingdom, the Kingdom of Israel: Bethel, Shechem, Penuel, and Mahanaim. (The revelation to Jacob in Beer-sheba, on his way to Egypt [46:1–4], was intended to portray him as having walked in the footsteps of his grandfather and father, for the same reason that the story of Abraham's wanderings opened with his appearances in Shechem and Bethel.)

The southern patriarchs and the northern patriarch were combined into one family, into a trinity of generations, in an effort to create one people, one nation that would unify south with north. This effort was sentenced to failure at a relatively early stage, however, when the unified kingdom of David and Solomon, which lasted less than a hundred years, collapsed into two separate dominions in the time of Jeroboam (who then ruled the northern Kingdom of Israel) and Rehoboam (who ruled the southern Kingdom of Judah). Abraham's "visits" in the northern cities and Jacob's "visit" to Beer-sheba were designed to endear one faction's holy cities to the inhabitants of the other, evidence, essentially, of the heated dispute between Judah and Israel over sacred real estate. The dispute is particularly apparent in Jacob's and Rachel's burial traditions: the Israelite tradition about Jacob's burial in Shechem (which we reconstructed) became replaced by the Judahite tradition that told of his burial in Hebron, a tradition that reflects the people of Judah's determination to claim Jacob's gravesite—a valuable political asset—to themselves. In the same way, the tradition about Rachel's burial in the territory of her son Benjamin (mentioned in 1 Samuel 10:2, and which we reconstructed), near Bethel, was rejected and replaced with an official one that told of her burial in David's birth city, Bethlehem. Both examples demonstrate the power wielded by the Judahite writers in the final shaping of the biblical historiography.

In Jacob's blessing of his sons, we noticed the reverse: a switch in Judah's blessing from "until he comes to Shalem [= Jerusalem; 49:10]" to "until he comes to Shiloh"—the city in the territory of Ephraim in which the primary temple in the waning of the period of the Judges was located (1 Sam 1:1 ff.). The Judah-Israel—actually, Judah-Joseph—polemic was also reflected in the account of the births of Jacob's sons, a story that contained two climaxes: the first, the birth of Judah, the fourth son of Leah, who proclaims: "This time I will praise the Lord" (Gen 29:35); and the second, at the end, when God remembered Rachel, Jacob's beloved, and she gave birth to Joseph.

We also found a twofold climax in the final edition of Jacob's blessing to his sons in Genesis 49, where Judah was blessed after his three older brothers had been cursed. He was given power and domination over his brothers: "Judah, you your brothers shall praise . . . your father's sons shall bow down to you" (v 8); but the blessing given Joseph ordains that he, and no other, was "elect of his brothers" (v 26).

We saw how decided effort was invested in exciting ill will against Shechem, the primary holy city in the territory of Ephraim. Dinah was raped by the Shechemites, and it was under the terebinth tree in Shechem that Jacob's household buried their idols on their way to Bethel (35:2a, 4), an expression of the polemic against a Shechemite tradition that told of Shechem's sanctity (Josh 24:26).

We saw also an inner-Israelite power struggle between Penuel (32:25–33) and Bethel (35:10–15), with each claiming to have been the site of a battle with a divine entity. We were able to reconstruct the tradition of a struggle taking place in Bethel with the help of a verse from outside the Pentateuch (Hos 12:4–5), and from a covert echo to the tradition in Genesis 35:13–15. The tradition that told of a struggle in Penuel did not remain in favor for long, owing to its mythical character, and was replaced by a tradition that told how, in Penuel, Jacob *saw* his brother and how seeing his face was "like seeing the face of God" (33:10), thereby providing a secular explanation for the city's name. A similar process occurred with the tradition about the sanctity of Mahanaim: a short, mild tradition admitted that *maḥaneh 'elohim*, "God's camp"—and not any sort of confrontation between God and Jacob—was located there (32:2–3), while in the same chapter we found a secularized etymology of the place-name that utterly detached it from the sacred: Jacob, fearing an attack by his brother, divided his household and property between two camps, *maḥanaim* (vv 8–11).

Indeed, this political war between holy cities extended beyond Israel's borders, to Babylon. The story of the stairway in Bethel (28:10–22), which Jacob realized was in fact heaven's gate, polemicized against a Babylonian tradition that had identified the gate to heaven with Babylon. The Samaritans, for whom Mount Gerizim in Shechem was considered to be the single legitimate holy site, would later claim that Bethel, in fact, is Shechem, while the Judahite midrashic tradition "transferred" Bethel to Jerusalem.

The Jacob stories also reflect Israel's relations with its neighbors. A tradition about the purchase of Shechem in Genesis 33:18–20 addressed another tradition, according to which Jacob had conquered Shechem "with sword and bow" (Gen 48:22), in order to teach readers that it was through proper legal, civil channels that the nation had acquired holdings in Israel. A later incident, in which the Hivites disguised themselves and tricked the Israelites and their leader, Joshua, in order to avoid massacre (Josh 9), was explained as redress—following the measure-for-measure principle—for the lethal treachery with which Jacob's sons deceived the Hivites/Shechemites.

In the Bible's depiction of the relationship between Jacob and Esau (Edom) we sense contours of actual relations between the nations of Israel and Edom, along with the ebb and flow in those relations. Biblical traditions that deal with later periods will return to these stories. When the Israelites return from Egypt after their years of slavery, the king of Edom refuses them passage, or even to sell them water (Num 20:14–21). The episode returns to the selling of the birthright for a bowl of lentil porridge (Gen 25:29–34). His anger still boiling despite the reconciliation between the brothers, Edom now takes revenge for having been forced to buy food from Jacob when he was hungry and exhausted. In the version in Deuteronomy, a book written, apparently, in a period of peaceful relations between the two countries, Edom is portrayed more favorably, agreeing to Israel's request to sell them food and water (2:28–29), thereby balancing the historical account between the two nations.

Israel's prophets—particularly those who were aware of

the Edomites' cooperation with the Babylonians in the latter's capture of Jerusalem and Judah—interpreted the Jacob stories in such a way that Jacob was entirely freed of guilt. Regarding Esau-Edom, not a drop of justification or defense was found (e.g., Isa 63:1–10; Obad 1:2; Mal 1:2–5). From these prophecies it is only a short leap to turn Edom into a monster, Israel's archenemy, and attach the identifying tag "Edom" or "Esau" onto any and every enemy that rises up against Israel in the course of history—a phenomenon known from rabbinic literature.

In the hands of biblical writers, contemporary relations between the nations of Israel and Aram, too, assumed the shape of the struggle between Jacob and Laban the Aramean. The tradition of the pact that was finally sealed between Jacob and Laban in Gilead, marking the border between them (Gen 31:44–54), was designed to support Israelite claims of territorial rights in Gilead during a period of bitter conflict over the region in the rule of Ahab (1 Kings 22:3) and his son Yehoram (2 Kings 9:14).

A view to the future is also apparent in the depiction of Jacob's punishment for cheating his father and brother. For that act of trickery, Jacob was punished with exile and slavery to Laban (shaped under the influence of the tradition about Israel's slavery in Egypt), which functions as a warning to future generations, a heavy-handed sign that the nation's immoral behavior is what will later lead to a similar fate. Israel's prophets made use of Jacob's deeds when they came to take account of the misbehavior of the nation (e.g., Isa 48:8; Jer 9:3–5). Micah, who knew the interpretation of the name Israel from *yashar,* "honest, righteous," which was intended, we recall, as a way to distance Jacob from the unflattering name by which he was known—one who cheats and deceives—claimed that Jacob had remained Jacob, *ya'aqov,* and that he (i.e., the nation) was undeserving of the name Israel (2:6–7).

Despite the unpleasant side of Jacob's character and the

punishments he must endure, the story of Jacob's life has another side, this one uplifting: God's favor never ceases to shine over Jacob, and the promise that was given to his predecessors, of fruitfulness and land, was also given to him (e.g., Gen 28:13–14). Jacob's frequently underhanded behavior did not preclude the realization of the divine plan. On the contrary, his many sons advanced the transformation of the patriarchal family into a nation—and yet they were the outcome of his many wives, who were, in turn, a direct effect of the lie with which he deceived his father. Jacob's partiality toward Joseph and the favoritism he showed his younger son, for which he was punished with Joseph's being torn from him, sold by his brothers and sent to Egypt, will, in the end, be revealed to have been a good thing, as expressed by Joseph when he reassured his brothers: "While you were intending evil toward me, God intended it for good, so as to bring this about, to keep alive an abundant people" (Gen 50:19–20).

Indeed, though God allows no transgression to be left unpunished, for educative purposes, in the end we can say with full confidence that he "intended it for good" and that there is yet reason to be optimistic following the bitter ending to the monarchical period, when the Israelites find themselves in Assyrian and Babylonian exile. The pages of history that are written later and the consoling words of Israel's prophets and poets expect good things for Jacob's descendants, the people of Israel: "O that from Zion may come Israel's deliverance; When the Lord restores the captured of his people, Jacob will exult, Israel will rejoice!" (Ps 14:7).

Abarbanel, Isaac, 23
Abimelech, 161
Abraham, 3–4, 161, 186; arriving in
  Canaan, 5; associated with altars
  in Shechem and Bethel, 119;
  burial of, 149, 177; commanded
  to go to Canaan, 79; defeat of
  Chedorlaomer, 134; God's promise
  to, 49–50; Lot parting from, 114
Absalom, 142
Acts
7: 15–16, 178
Aggadat Bereshit: 52, 136
altar, commemorating connection
  between Bethel and Jerusalem,
  58–59
Amnon, 124
Amos
3: 12, 87
7: 13, 54
angels, 48; two groups of, 50; unnamed,
  102

Araunah, 118
Asher, Jacob's blessing of, 173–74

Babylon, Bethel contrasted to, 54
Babylonian myth, Temple of Marduk,
  55
barren women, 14–15, 66
Beer-sheba, 4, 160, 161–62, 177, 186
Benjamin, 157–59; birth of, 136, 138,
  141; Jacob's blessing of, 174, 176;
  tribe of, 141, 176
Bethel, 52, 54, 105–6, 107–8, 109,
  119–20, 129–31, 132, 138; blessing
  of, 57; contrasted to Babylon, 54;
  destruction of, 57–58; identified
  with Jerusalem, 58–59
Bethlehem, 139, 141
Beth-on, 106, 137–38
Bible: accumulating similar words and
  expressions to connect texts, 42–43;
  biblical heroes in, birth stories of,
  14; biographies in, purpose of,

Bible (*continued*)
185–86; championing territorial
convictions, 186; depicting Israel's
history through biography, 11;
duplicate traditions in, 9; imperfec-
tion of heroes in, 10–11; impersonators in, paying for their deception,
31; inverse relationships appearing
in, 85; isolationist ideology of, 5,
13; literary genres of, 10; midrash
appearing in, 10; providing foundation for other literature, 9–10;
skipping years between birth
and adulthood, 21; as source for
biography, 7–8; three-four pattern
in, 67; two megaevents of, 4
Bilhah, 66, 69–70, 137, 141–45
biography: Bible's approach to, 8,
185–86; depicting Israel's history
through, 11; sources for, 7–8
birthright, stealing of, 19. *See also*
Jacob: purchasing Esau's birthright
birth stories, 14
Blessing of Jacob, 169–70
blessings, 101; importance of, 29. *See
also* Jacob: blessing his sons before
his death
Bokhim, 107, 109, 138
Bordeaux pilgrim, 109, 139
burials, serving political purposes,
179–80
burnt offerings, 58–59

Canaan, 3, 4; as ancestral burial site,
177; famine in, 157; God commanding a return to, 79, 88–89; Jacob's
desire to be buried in, 176–77; land
acquisitions in, 118; length of time
the patriarchs resided in, 163; patriarchs' journey in, significance of, 5–7
Chronicles, Reuben's account in,
147–48
1 Chronicles
1: 37, 19
4: 9–10, 138; *24–43*, 171
5: 1–3, 147
7: 28, 138

17: 21, 59
21: 58; *22–25*, 118; *26*, 58
22: 1, 58
concubines, sons' sexual relations with
their fathers', 142–43
Covenant between the Pieces, 6
Creation, opening point for Israel's
history, 2–3

Dan, Jacob's blessing of, 173–74
daughters of the land, significance of
term, 126
David, 172; escape from King Saul, 85;
standing at juncture between earth
and heaven, 59
deceit, 84
Deuteronomy, 170
2: 4, 25; *6*, 25; *28–29*, 25, 189
5: 15, 4
13: 2, 47
15: 13, 87
16: 21–22, 52
21: 17, 147
22: 6–7, 98
23: 8, 25
26: 14, 137–38
27: 5–6, 120; *20*, 145
32: 8–11, 1–2; *15*, 110
33: 29, 170; *5*, 110; *6*, 171; *13*, 36;
    13–16, 175; *19*, 173; *20*, 174; *26*, 110
Dinah, 74; story of, 120–29, 172
disguise, as literary method, 31
divination, 77, 82, 159
divine retribution, 7, 11
dreams, 83; Joseph's, 153–54; relating
to other dreams, 80–81; as vehicles
for prophecy, 47

Edom, 16, 17, 19, 23, 31; condemnation of, 26–27; hatred toward, 44;
negative portrayal of, in Numbers,
25; relations with Israel, 24–27;
revenge against, prophecy of, 41–44;
status of, 26
Egypt, patriarchs sentenced to
servitude in, 163
El-Elohei-Israel, 118, 119

"Enuma Elish," 55–56
Ephraim, 165–68
Esau: bestial nature of, 22–24; birth of, 17–20; burying his father, 149; learning of the stolen blessing, 34–36; receiving Isaac's blessing, 36–38; reunited with Jacob, 96–97, 104, 110–13; selling the birthright, 23–24; settling separately from Jacob, 114; unworthiness of, 39, 40–41, 44
Eusebius, 117
Exodus (book of), 170
1: 12, 88
3: 7–8, 89; *22*, 89
4: 24–26, 100
7: 16, 89
12: 2, 2; 26, 89; *40*, 163
14: 5, 89; *7–8*, 90
15: 6, 138
19: 10, 130; *14*, 130
20: 11, 4
22: 12, 86–87
23: 15, 104
34: 20, 104
Exodus (event), 4; story of, influencing the story of Jacob leaving Laban's house, 88–90
Ezekiel
21: 26, 82
Ezra, anti-Samaritan agenda of, 60
4: 60; 1, 60; *2*, 60; *3*, 60

force, patriarchs' use of, 134–35
fraternal conflict, 15–18
fruitfulness, as blessing, 33, 36–37, 45, 164, 167, 171

Gad, Jacob's blessing of, 174
Genesis, 142, 170; assigning Israel's place, 3–4; first stories in, purpose of, 1–4; portraying patriarchs as men of peace, 134; story of Dinah in, without secondary additions, 122–24, 142
3: 3
4: 1–2, 21; 20, 21
5: 1, 3

9: 20–27, 144
10: 1, 3; 6, 3; 17, 126
11: 1–9, 3, 54; 2, 56; 3, 56; 3–4, 55; 4, 54; 5, 56; 8, 57; 8–9, 57; 9, 54; 10ff., 3–4
12: 1, 5, 50, 79; 3, 34, 50; 4, 163; *4–5*, 105–6; *6*, 51; *6–8*, 119, 186; *8*, 119; *9*, 186; *10–20*, 121; *20*, 121; *12:20–13:1*, 6
13: 5–12, 15, 114; *7–12*, 134; *14–16, 49–50*
14: 14–17, 134; *18–20*, 117
15: 6; 16, 6
16: 14; 20, 15; 26, 15
17: 5, 102; *15–16*, 102
18: 2, 100; *16*, 100; *18*, 172; *22*, 100
19: 1, 100; *5*, 100; *8*, 100; *10*, 100; *12*, 100; *15*, 100; *16*, 100; *30–37*, 144
21: 161; 5, 163; *10, 15; 22, 15, 16, 17; 23, 16, 17; 24, 17; 25, 17; 25–32*, 134; *26, 17; 27–34, 17; 30*, 161; *31*, 161
22: 17, 75, 98
23: 177; 8–20, 118; *10–15*, 77
24: 3, 13, 39; 12–14, 13; 18, 14; 50, 14; 67, 14
25: 7–9, 149; *9–10*, 177; *19–26*, 7; *20, 14; 21, 14; 22, 18, 39; 23, 24, 27, 34, 37; 25, 30; 26, 35*, 149, 163; *27, 21, 33, 47; 27–29*, 177; *28, 22, 28, 29*, 149; *29, 72; 29–30, 22; 29–34*, 189; *30, 23, 72; 31, 23, 73; 32, 23, 73; 33, 24; 33–34, 73; 34, 24, 27, 34*
26: 39; 1–2, 161; *1–13*, 121; *13, 32; 21*, 161; *24*, 161; *25*, 161; *30*, 92; *31*, 161; *34, 31; 34–35*, 39
27: 28, 42; 1, 28, 165; *1–4*, 149; *27:1–28:9*, 149; *3, 33; 4, 29; 5, 29; 8–10, 29; 11–12, 30; 13, 30; 15, 42; 15–16, 30; 18, 32; 19, 32; 20, 32; 21, 32; 22, 33; 23, 33; 24, 33; 25, 33; 26–27, 33; 27, 33; 28, 33; 29, 33–34, 37*, 111; *30, 34, 43; 32, 34; 33, 34–35; 34, 35; 35, 35, 64*, 127; *36, 35; 37, 35–36; 38, 36; 39–40, 36; 40, 43; 41, 37, 43, 44; 42, 27, 37–38, 43; 43–44, 63; 43–45, 38; 44*, 148, 156; *44–45, 43; 46, 39*, 126, 148

Genesis (cont.)

28: 56; *1*, 39; *1–2*, 40; *3–4*, 40; *4*, 49;
   6, 40; *6–7*, 40; *8–9*, 40; *10*, 6; *10–22*,
   188–89; *11*, 47, 51, 59, 95; *12*, 47,
   48; *13*, 48, 49, 56, 97; *13–14*, 191;
   14, 50, 57, 98; *15*, 50, 52, 53, 57, 79–
   80, 97; *16*, 50; *17*, 51, 52, 57, 58; *18*,
   51, 56, 59; *19*, 52, 57; *20–21*, 53, 117;
   20–22, 52; *21*, 53; *22*, 54, 56, 57, 59
29: *1*, 56, 61; *2*, 61; *6*, 62; *15*, 62;
   16–17, 62; *18*, 63; *19*, 63; *20*, 63; *21*,
   63; *24*, 66; *25*, 63, 78; *26–27*, 64; *27*,
   65; *29*, 66; *30*, 65; *31*, 66, 153; *32*,
   66; *33*, 67, 153; *34*, 67; *35*, 67, 187
30: 81, 136; *1*, 68, 75, 136, 185; *2*,
   68; *3*, 69; *4*, 69; *6*, 69–70; *8*, 70; *9*,
   70; *11*, 70; *13*, 70; *14*, 71, 72, 143;
   14–18, 143; *15*, 71, 73; *16*, 71, 73,
   185; *17–18*, 72; *19*, 73; *20*, 73; *21*,
   74; *22–23*, 74; *23*, 75, 152; *24*, 75,
   137; *25*, 76, 89; *26*, 76; *27–28*, 77;
   29, 77; *30*, 77; *31*, 77–78; *32–33*, 78;
   34, 78; *37*, 81; *39*, 79; *42*, 79; *43*,
   79, 88
31: 81; *1*, 79; *3*, 79, 97; *6–7*, 80; *8*,
   80; *9*, 80, 89; *10–12*, 80; *12–13*, 89,
   95; *13*, 52, 80–81, 90; *14–16*, 81;
   15–16, 83; *17–18*, 82; *19*, 83, 131,
   159; *19–20*, 82; *20*, 83; *20–21*, 89;
   22, 89–90; *23*, 159; *24*, 83; *25*, 90,
   159; *26–28*, 83; *29*, 83, 87; *30*, 82,
   84, 159; *31*, 84; *32*, 84, 137, 159;
   33, 84; *34*, 84; *34–35*, 159; *35*, 84;
   36–37, 86; *36–42*, 160; *38–39*, 86;
   40, 87; *41*, 76, 87; *42*, 87; *43*, 88;
   31:43–32:1, 159; *44–54*, 190; *45*, 90;
   47, 90; *49*, 90; *50*, 91; *51–53*, 91
32: *1*, 92; *1–2*, 111; *2*, 92, 94, 95, 152;
   2–3, 94, 188; *2b–3*, 103; *3*, 111; *4*,
   111; *5*, 96, 112; *6*, 96; *6–7*, 112; *7*,
   96; *8*, 112, 113; *8–9*, 97; *8–11*, 188;
   9, 112; *10*, 97, 112, 113; *11*, 97,
   113; *12*, 98; *13*, 98; *13–14*, 113; *14*,
   98; *14–21*, 99; *15*, 113; *15–16*, 98;
   16–17, 113; *17*, 99; *18–21*, 99; *19*,
   98, 112; *21*, 98, 104, 112; *22*, 98, 99;
   23ff., 6; *23–25*, 100; *25*, 100; *25–33*,

188; *26*, 100; *26–30*, 101; *27*, 101,
   106; *27–30b*, 101; *29*, 100, 102, 106,
   109; *30*, 106, 108; *30a*, 102; *31*, 103
33–35: 116
33: *1*, 111; *10*, 104, 188; *18*, 116, 133;
   18–20, 133, 135, 178, 189; *19*, 118,
   119, 133; *20*, 118
34: 122–25, 126, 172; *1*, 126; *2*, 122,
   125; *2a*, 126; *3*, 122, 126; *4*, 126; *5*,
   122; *7*, 122, 125; *7b*, 122; *8–10*, 126;
   11–12, 127; *13*, 122, 127; *13a*, 127;
   14–16, 127; *17*, 122; *18*, 127; *19*, 127;
   20–21, 127; *22*, 127; *23*, 127; *24*, 127;
   25–26, 122; *25–26a*, 128; *26b*, 122;
   27, 122; *27a*, 128; *28–29*, 128; *30*,
   122; *30–31*, 128; *31*, 122, 128
35: 109, 129, 131–32, 144, 146,
   148; *1–4*, 129–31; *2*, 131; *2a*, 188;
   2b, 130; *4*, 130, 131, 132, 188; *5*,
   128–29; *7*, 52; *8*, 107, 109; *9–15*,
   108, 165; *10*, 110; *10–11*, 108;
   10–15, 188; *11–12*, 164; *13*, 108;
   13–15, 188; *14*, 108; *15*, 108; *16*,
   136; *16–20*, 136, 160, 165; *17*,
   136; *17–20*, 85; *18*, 137, 138; *19*,
   141; *19–20*, 139; *21–22*, 125, 171;
   21–22a, 141; *22*, 143, 171; *22b–26*,
   141; *23*, 147; *23–26*, 146; *27*, 144,
   148; *28–29*, 148, 149; *29*, 114
36: 114; *6–8*, 114; *8*, 17; *17*, 19
37–48: 176
37: *2*, 151, 152, 154; *3*, 152, 153; *4*,
   153; *7*, 153; *8*, 153; *9*, 153; *10*, 154;
   11, 154, 156; *13*, 154; *14*, 133, 154;
   31–32, 155; *33*, 155; *34*, 156; *35*,
   156, 158, 161, 165
38: 18–19; *27–30*, 19
39: *3*, 151–52
41: 157
42: *4*, 157; *36*, 157; *37*, 158; *38*, 158
43: *9*, 158; *14*, 158
44: *4*, 159; *5*, 159; *6*, 159; *9*, 159; *12*,
   159; *14*, 160; *15*, 159, 160; *16*, 160;
   18–34, 160; *34*, 160
45: *1–3*, 160; *1–15*, 159; *3*, 160; *8*, 160;
   9, 160; *26*, 160; *28*, 162; *45:28–46:1*,
   161

46: 1, 161; *1–4*, 186; *2–3*, 161; *4*, 162,
  177; *7ff.*, 6; *23*, 173; *29*, 162; *30*, 162
47: 9, 162; *12*, 164; *27*, 164; *28*, 162;
  29–31, 164, 176; *29–32*, 176–77
48: 135, 164; *1*, 164; *4*, 164; *5*, 165; *7*,
  139, 165; *10*, 165; *13*, 166; *14*, 166;
  15, 175; *15–16*, 166; *17–18*, 166–67;
  19, 167; *20*, 167; *22*, 119, 133,
  134–35, 189
49: 29, 125, 128, 146, 148; *1*, 169; *2*,
  170; *3*, 137, 147; *3–4*, 146; *3–15*,
  170; *4*, 171; *5*, 171; *5–7*, 125, 172;
  6, 171; *7*, 171; *8*, 172, 187–88; *8–10*,
  175; *10*, 172, 187; *13*, 172–73;
  14–15, 173; *15*, 173; *16*, 173; *16–18*,
  170; *17*, 174; *19*, 174; *19–20*, 170;
  20, 174; *21*, 170; *22*, 175; *22–23*,
  170; *23*, 175; *24*, 175; *25–26*,
  175–76; *25b–26*, 175; *26*, 188; *26b*,
  175; *27*, 176; *28*, 169; *33*, 177;
  49:33–50:14, 7
50: 176; *1*, 177; *2–3*, 177; *5*, 178; *7–9*,
  180; *13*, 179; *17*, 68; *19*, 68; *19–20*,
  191; *20*, 69
Genesis Rabbah
64: 11, 154
65: 18, 32; *19*, 32–33
68: 12, 50
70: 17, 64–65
74: 32, 137
79: 7, 119
81: 3, 132
82: 9, 140
98: 4, 142
Gibeah, concubine of, 107–8
God: balancing the books, 65–66,
  128, 191; blessing Joseph, 164;
  commanding a return to Canaan,
  79–80, 88–89; commanding
  Jacob to erect an altar in Bethel,
  129–30; confrontation with, 102–3;
  contrasted in stories of Jacob's
  dream and the Tower of Babel,
  56; different character of, in
  Joseph's story, 151–52; freeing
  female members of a patriarchal
  family, 121; opening Rachel's womb,
  74; promising Jacob protection
  on all future paths, 52–53;
  providence of, 87; revealing
  himself to Jacob in Beer-sheba,
  161–62, 177, 186; role of, in
  Leah's pregnancy and birth, 66;
  tempering Laban's anger, 83
gods, alien, removing from Bethel,
  130, 131–32
Goshen, 163–64
guerrilla warfare, 174

Hamor, 127–28
Haran, society of, 64, 65
heaven's gate, transferred from Babylon
  to Bethel to Jerusalem, 55–58
Hebron, 118, 119
hero, confronting the divine/demonic
  at a crossing point, 100
Hivites, 126
Hosea, 108; explaining Jacob's name,
  18, 20; interpreting names of Jacob,
  Israel, and Bethel, 106
3: 2, 178
12: 109; *4*, 18, 105, 106, 137; *4–5*, 188;
  5, 107

Iliad: 9.448–57, 142–43
impersonators, paying for their
  deception, 31
Isaac, 148, 161, 186; advancing age
  of, 28, 32–33; blessing Esau, 36–38,
  39; blessing Jacob, 33–34, 40, 49;
  blindness of, 28, 32–33, 165–66;
  death and burial of, 149, 177;
  favoritism of, 22; greeting Jacob
  on his return, 149
Isaiah, prophecy of revenge against
  Esau/Edom, 41–44
1: 18, 19; *24*, 43
40–66: 41
44: 2, 110
48: 1, 110; *8*, 20, 190
49: 7, 108
63: 1, 42, 43; *1–6*, 41–42; *1–10*, 190; *2*,
  42; *3*, 43; *4*, 43; *6*, 43
65: 11, 70

Israel (Jacob): name of, interpreted, 106; name change to, 108–10; transformation of, 169

Israel (nation): blamed for deceitful behavior, 20–21; border with Aram, 91–92; destruction of, 3; first reference to, 173–74; gathering the tribes of, 131; genealogy of, 3–4; growth of, 88; history of, starting point, 1–3; isolationism of, 164; patriarchal stories, purpose of, 4–7; prevented from entering the world prematurely, 3; relations with Edom, 16, 24–27; return to Canaan, 5–6; rivalry with Judah, 179–80, 187; separate from Canaanite culture, 5; tribes of, 66; unique culture of, 4

Issachar, Jacob's blessing of, 173

Jacob: age of, on arrival in Egypt, 162–63; angels accompanying, 95; answering Laban's deceit, 78–79; as archetype for Israel, 10; arriving in Egypt, 162–63; arriving in Shechem, 116–18; becoming the founder of a nation, 169; birth of, 17–20; births of his sons, stories containing two climaxes, 187; blamelessness of, 21–22, 24; blessing Asher, 173–74; blessing Benjamin, 174, 176; blessing Dan, 173–74; blessing Ephraim and Manasseh, 166–68; blessing Gad, 174; blessing his sons before his death, 169–76, 187–88; blessing Issachar, 173; blessing Joseph, 172, 174–76; blessing Judah, 171, 172, 174, 175; blessing Naphtali, 173–74; blessing Zebulun, 172–73; blindness of, 165, 167; building an altar in Bethel, 129–31; burial of, 176–79, 187; burying his father, 149; character of, 184–85, 190–91; cheating Esau in utero, tradition of, 18, 20; chosen status of, 45; claiming divine intervention in actions against Laban, 80–81; conquering territo-

ries with a sword and bow, 134–35; contributing to Rachel's death, 137; cursing his three eldest sons from his deathbed, 125, 128, 146, 170–72; death of, 177; deception story of, influencing biblical writers, 41–45; demonstrating little initiative in the Shechem stories, 135; describing God as his shepherd, 175; disassociating, from deceit and cheating, 109–10; discovering his marriage to Leah, 63–64; dispatched to Haran, 40–41, 46–47; doing Rebekah's bidding, 29–31; dreams of, 47–54, 56–57, 80–81, 95, 153–54; encountering angels at Mahanaim, 94–96; encouraging Joseph's tattling, 155; entering pact with Laban, 90–92; enumerating his work for Laban, 86–87; exonerated for stealing the blessing, 29–30; expecting fulfillment of God's promises, 52–53; facing consequences for buying the birthright, 25; failing as a father, 185; favoritism toward Joseph, revealed as a good thing, 191; fear of, following his dream, 51; giving commands about his burial and grave, 176–77; God revealed to, in Beer-sheba, 161–62, 177, 186; grieving for Joseph, 156–57; indifferent to Dinah, 120, 121, 127, 128; indifferent to Rachel's pain, 68–69; journey to Haran undescribed, 61; learning that Joseph is alive, 160–61; leaving Haran for Canaan, 82, 92; leaving Laban, 94; lies of, writers trying to neutralize, 32; linked to the temple, 54; love of, for Rachel, 61–63, 65; mandrake story reflecting his purchase of the birthright, 72–73; meeting Rachel, 62; meeting with Joseph before his death, 164–65; mourning period for, 180; naming Bethel, 52; naming of, explanations for, 18, 20–21; nature of, decided in the womb, 20–21;

negatively summarizing his own life, 162–63; passiveness of, 31, 69, 70, 71–73, 75, 152; preferring independence from Esau, 113–14; preparing to reunite with Esau, 93–94, 96–99, 104; prophets interpreting the stories of, 10; punished for his actions, 38–39, 64–65, 156; purchasing Esau's birthright, 17, 21, 22–24, 53; purchasing land in Shechem, 118; reacting to Reuben's actions with Bilhah, 146; receiving blessing from God, 164; relying on magic rather than God, 79; renamed Israel, 93, 101–2, 108–10; requesting support for journey to Haran, 50, 52; responding to Laban's accusations of theft, 84; returning to his father's home, 148; reunited with Esau, 104, 110–13; reunited with Joseph, 162; sensing death approaching, 164; setting up pillar as house of God, 51–54, 56–57; settling in Goshen, 163–64; sons of, actions in Shechem, 123–28; sons' genealogy, 146–47; speaking with the spirit of prophecy, 167, 169, 180; stealing the blessing from Esau, 28, 32–34, 53; stories about, opposing forces at work in, 11–12; struggling with God's representatives, tradition of, 95–96, 105–6; transforming into Israel, 169; travels of, 6; treating Joseph as the favorite, 152–53; vast world opening before, 49; wanting to be buried in Canaan, 176–77; wanting to preserve priority of the younger son, 164–68; wanting to return to Canaan, 76–77, 79, 94; wives of, casting a long shadow on the future, 75; wrestling with adversary before reuniting with Esau, 100–101; wrestling with God, 102

jealousy: Joseph's brothers', 153–55; Laban's sons', 79; Leah's sons', 152; Rachel's, toward Leah, 67–68, 70, 75; between Sarah and Hagar, 69

Jeremiah: prophecy about Edom, 26–27; using Jacob-Esau relationship to illustrate deceit, 20–21
7: 12, 172
9: 3–5, 20–21, 190
17: 25, 108
31: 15, 140; 15–17, 138; 29, 159
48: 13, 52
49: 15, 26
Jerusalem, 118, 119, 172; Bethel identified with, 58–59; sanctification of, 58
Joseph, 68, 69, 111; birth of, 74–75, 76; brothers' hatred of, 153, 154–56; burial place of, 118, 119; disappearance of, 137; dreams of, 153–54; inheriting Reuben's birthright, 147; intervening in blessing of his sons, 166–67; Jacob's blessing of, 172, 174–76; Jacob's stories casting a long shadow over, 152; meeting with Jacob before his death, 164–65; Moses' blessing to, 175–76; planning to bury Jacob in Shechem, 178; reunited with Jacob, 162; rise of, 151; serving the sons of Jacob's concubines, 152; Shechem promised to, 134; story of, literary quality of, 151–52; supporting family during the famine, 164; testing his brothers, 157–60
Joshua
5: 9, 127
8: 30ff., 120
9: 128, 189; 10–16, 173
18: 12, 106; 22, 138; 25, 140
19: 1, 171; 47, 174
24: 131–32; 4, 115; 12, 134; 23, 131; 26, 131, 188; 32, 118, 133, 134, 178
Joshua ben Nun, 6
Jubilees, 143; explaining expansion of Jacob's flock, 81; retelling biblical stories to provide support for certain laws, 145; separating Shalem and Shechem, 117
19: 13, 21–22

Jubilees (cont.)
28: 25–26, 81
30: 1, 117; 17, 129; 23, 129
33: 1–10, 144–45
Judah (nation), 3, 141; acquiring land in, 118; Judah-Israel rivalry, 179–80, 187
Judah (son of Jacob), 18–19, 160; birth of, 67, 75; Jacob's blessing of, 126, 146, 171, 172, 174, 175
Judges
1: 10, 119
2: 1–5, 107
6: 22, 103
8: 17, 105
11: 29, 90
13: 17–18, 102; 25, 174
15: 18, 127
18: 25, 95; 27–29, 174
20–21: 107
20: 23, 107; 26, 107
21: 1, 107
Judith
8: 1, 129
9: 2–3, 129

Kings
1 Kings
2: 11, 179
4: 14, 95
8: 46, 11
12: 25, 105, 133, 179
16: 24, 118
22: 3, 91, 190
2 Kings
8: 20, 37
9: 14, 91, 190
14: 8–11, 103
16: 6, 37
17: 6, 6; 24–33, 60
23: 15–18, 57
25: 21, 6

Laban: consenting to Rachel's marriage to Jacob, 63; entering pact with Jacob, 90–92; family of, 62; idol of, 82–83; modeled after Pharaoh,

88, 90; offering to pay Jacob, 77–79; pursuing Jacob, 83; sons of, jealous of Jacob, 79; tricking Jacob, 63–65
Lamentations
4: 21–22, 26
land acquisition, 118
Law of Retribution, 87
Leah, 62; burial of, 177; competing with Rachel, 66–67, 70–74; discussing leaving Haran with Jacob, 80, 81–82; God opening the womb of, 66; married to Jacob, 63–66
Levi, 122, 125, 128–29, 171–72
Leviticus
18: 8, 145
20: 11, 145
literary archaeology, 9–10

Machpelah, 118, 178, 179
Mahanaim, 94–96, 98, 103, 104–5, 113
maidservants, 65–66
Malachi: bitterness regarding the Edomites, 27; prophecy about Esau/Edom, 44–45
1: 2–5, 27, 44, 190
Manasseh, 165–68
mandrakes, significance of, 71, 72–73, 143
Meir (Rabbi), 141
Micah, speaking angrily at false prophets, 36–37
2: 6–7, 190
2: 7, 109
3: 6, 36
Michal, 85–86
midrash, 10
Midrash HaGadol, 18
Monotheistic Manifesto, 4
Moses: blessing Joseph, 175–76; commanding erection of an altar in Shechem, 120
Mount Gilead, 90

names: changes in, linked with threatening confrontations, 102, 105–6;

etymology of, 18, 23, 30, 35, 52, 54,
57, 58, 66–67, 70, 72, 73–75, 90, 96,
97, 98, 103–5, 107, 109, 112–13,
116–17, 138, 166–67, 173, 174;
linked with destiny, 102
Naphtali, Jacob's blessing of, 173–74
narrative efficiency, 153
negotiating practices, 77–78
Nehemiah
  11: 13, 140
"Nergal and Ereshkigal," 48
Numbers, wanting to portray Edom
  negatively, 25
8: 7, 130
20: 14, 25; *14–21*, 189; *17*, 25; *18*, 25;
  19, 25; *20–21*, 25
23: 8, 45; *9*, 5; *10*, 109

Obadiah, on the Edomites and their
  betrayal, 26
1: 2, 26, 190
11: 26
Onomasticon (Eusebius), 117

patriarchs, artificial structure of,
  186–87
Peniel, 103
Penuel, 103–6, 112
Perez, 18–20
Pesikta Rabbati: 13, 113
Pharaoh, Laban modeled after, 88, 90
pillars, 51–52; erected at pact between
  Jacob and Laban, 90–91; foundation
  for God's house, 56–57, 59; functioning as protection and witnesses,
  91
Pirkei de-Rabbi Eliezer: 35, 59
property, just division of, 114–15
prophecy, dreams as vehicles for, 47
prophets, interpreting stories about
  Jacob, 10
Proverbs
7: 18, 71
Psalms
7: 16, 178
12: 3, 30

14: 7, 191
60: 8, 133
63: 2, 22
76: 2–3, 117; *3*, 172
78: 6off., 172
106: 6–7, 2
107: 8–9, 29
108: 8, 133
111: 6, 2
136: 7–11, 4–5
137: 26; *7*, 26

Rachel: burial of, 138–41, 179, 187;
  death of, 136–38, 141, 142, 165;
  God opening the womb of, 74;
  jealous of Leah, 67–72, 74–75, 136;
  leaving Haran, 80, 81, 83; meeting
  Jacob, 62; most precious to Jacob,
  111; stealing her father's terafim,
  82–86, 159–60
Radak (Rabbi David Kimhi), 16
Rashi (Rabbi Shlomo Itzhaki), 2, 5, 16,
  19, 133
Rebekah: absence of, at Jacob's return,
  148–49; birth of sons, 15–17;
  burial of, 177; egocentrism of, 38;
  inadvertent prophecies of, 148;
  instructing Jacob to steal Isaac's
  blessing, 29–31; love of, for Jacob,
  22; planning Jacob's escape, 38;
  punished for her deception, 38
reconstruction, of traditions, 8–9
Reuben, 71, 72, 125, 126, 141–47, 152,
  171–72
Ruth
4: 18–22, 19

Sabbath, commandment related to,
  4–5
Samaria, 118, 119
Samaritans, 59, 117, 132
Samuel
  1 Samuel, 86
1–4: 172
1: 1ff., 187
10: 2, 139, 187

Samuel (cont.)
13: 5, 106
14: 23, 106
17: 36, 127
19: 11–17, 85
22: 2, 96
25: 13, 96
28: 6, 47
30: 10, 96
2 Samuel
2: 8, 95
5: 6–8, 119
6: 23, 86
11: 145
13: 124, 125; *12*, 125; *13*, 125; *14*, 125; 21, 125
16: 21–22, 142
17: 24ff., 95
20: 3, 142
21: 14, 140
23: 3, 175
24: 58; 21–24, 118
Sarah, burial of, 177
Saul, burial of, 140
Seir, 30. *See also* Edom
Shalem, 116–18, 172, 180
shechem, 133–34
Shechem (place), 60, 116–21, 130, 131–35, 178–79
Shechem (son of Hamor), 120–21, 122, 126–27
Shechemites, circumcision of, 120–21, 127–28
Shiloh, 172, 180
sibling rivalry, 72, 166. *See also* fraternal conflict
Sifre Deuteronomy: 352, 141
Simeon, 122, 125, 128–29, 171–72
Song of Moses, 1–2
Song of Songs
7: 13–14, 71
stairways, 48–49, 51, 56
Succoth, 113–14
sword of divine origin, 129

Tamar, 18–19, 124
Tanḥuma: Buber: Mikets: *13*, 160; Toledot: 10, 32; Vayeshev: 2, 133; Vayetse: 12, 82
Targum Onkelos, 133
Targum Pseudo-Jonathan, 134
temple: founding myth of, 54; rebuilding of, 59–60
Temple of Marduk, 55
terafim, 82–85, 131
terebinth, 131
Testament of Gad
1: 4–5, 154
Testament of Joseph
20: 6, 179
Testament of Levi
5: 2–3, 129
Testament of Reuben, 143–45
3: 9–15, 143–44
Testaments of the Twelve Patriarchs, 143–45, 154
Testament of Zebulun
4: 10–11, 155–56
theft, 82–83
three-four pattern, 67, 146, 170–71
Tosefta Sota: 11.13, 140
Tower of Babel, 54–57
traditions: duplicate, 9; reconstruction of, 8–9
Tseltsaḥ, 139–40
twins, birth stories of, 15–20

violence, for sake of pleasure, 171

womb, opening of, 14–15, 66, 74
words, power in, 29

Yeshurun, 110

Zebulun, Jacob's blessing of, 172–73
Zechariah
10: 2, 82
Zerah, 18–19

ALSO IN THE SERIES:

Sarah: The Life of Sarah Bernhardt, by Robert Gottlieb
Moshe Dayan: Israel's Controversial Hero, by Mordechai Bar-On
Emma Goldman: Revolution as a Way of Life, by Vivian Gornick
Hank Greenberg: The Hero Who Didn't Want to Be One, by Mark
     Kurlansky
Moses Mendelssohn: Sage of Modernity, by Shmuel Feiner
Walter Rathenau: Weimar's Fallen Statesman, by Shulamit Volkov
Solomon: The Lure of Wisdom, by Steven Weitzman
Leon Trotsky: A Revolutionary's Life, by Joshua Rubenstein

FORTHCOMING TITLES INCLUDE:

David Ben-Gurion, by Anita Shapira
Bernard Berenson, by Rachel Cohen
Irving Berlin, by James Kaplan
Leonard Bernstein, by Allen Shawn
Louis Brandeis, by Jeffrey Rosen
Martin Buber, by Paul Mendes-Flohr
Benjamin Disraeli, by David Cesarani
Bob Dylan, by Ron Rosenbaum
Sigmund Freud, by Adam Phillips
George Gershwin, by Gary Giddins
Ben Hecht, by Adina Hoffman
Heinrich Heine, by Fritz Stern
Lillian Hellman, by Dorothy Gallagher

Theodor Herzl, by Derek Penslar
Vladimir Jabotinsky, by Hillel Halkin
Franz Kafka, by Saul Friedlander
Abraham Isaac Kook, by Yehudah Mirsky
Primo Levi, by Berel Lang
Groucho Marx, by Lee Siegel
J. Robert Oppenheimer, by David Rieff
Marcel Proust, by Benjamin Taylor
Rashi, by Jack Miles
Mark Rothko, by Annie Cohen-Solal
Jonas Salk, by David Margolick
Steven Spielberg, by Molly Haskell
Ludwig Wittgenstein, by Anthony Gottlieb